how to improve your marriage without talking about it

how to improve your marriage without talking about it

Finding Love Beyond Words

PATRICIA LOVE, ED.D., and
STEVEN STOSNY, PH.D.

BROADWAY BOOKS

New York

PUBLISHED BY BROADWAY BOOKS

Published in the United States by Broadway Books, an imprint of
The Doubleday Broadway Publishing Group, a division of Random House, Inc., New York.
www.broadwaybooks.com

BROADWAY BOOKS and its logo, a letter B bisected on the diagonal,
are trademarks of Random House, Inc.

Illustrations by Meredith Hamilton
Book design by Nicola Ferguson

Library of Congress Cataloging-in-Publication Data
Love, Patricia.
    How to improve your marriage without talking about it : finding love beyond words / by
Patricia Love, Steven Stosny. — 1st ed.
        p. cm.
1. Marriage. 2. Interpersonal relations. I. Stosny, Steven. II. Title.

HQ734.L7556 2007
646.7'8—dc22

                                2006012147

ISBN: 978-0-7679-2317-0

PRINTED IN THE UNITED STATES OF AMERICA

10   9   8   7   6   5   4   3

To Terrie Chase, who has no idea
how supportive
she has been over the years.
—Pat Love

To my mother, Barbara McCrocklin.
—Steve Stosny

contents

acknowledgments

To Kathleen McFadden, whose third eye, dogged demand for clarity, and enormous writing talent were a vital part of this book, special thanks for the endless hours she spent slogging through every word of every page. To Kris Puopolo—okay, this is where I get emotional, because writing has been the single scariest thing I've ever done. Her support, encouragement, and enthusiasm have given me the courage to continue to write despite the fact that I am only an author, not a writer. Not only that, she took a manuscript that was fifty-five thousand words too long and made it into a book without losing one important fact. Her editing made this the juicy, polished product that it is. To Jim Levine, who has been my fantasy agent, gratitude for the enormous amount of personal time and energy he put into every single aspect of this book. To Suzie Bolotin, for giving us the title of this book. And finally, because this book was due right about the time Hurricane Katrina hit and, it just so happened, at the same time an emotional hurricane hit my life, I want to thank the friends who held me up during the period my world was falling down.

—Pat Love

I can only double every bit of gratitude Pat expressed for Kathleen, Kris, Jim, and Suzie. Producing this book was an exhilarating experience because of them. As always, my ultimate inspiration came from my mother, Barbara

McCrocklin, and from Christine and Carmen, who made me believe, in different ways, that I could be a good person. I am also grateful to the thousands of clients who have inspired me with their courage and their willingness to change old habits that obscured the compassionate people they were. I owe a special thanks to Stephanie, for emotional support during the difficult stages of writing. And finally, I am grateful to the many pets I have had, who made me curious to investigate ethological research on the emotions of social animals, which are important in understanding our own. They were and are great companions, too.

—*Steven Stosny*

authors' note

The studies that support this book, like all research, are about *group averages,* not individuals. The gender studies tell us a lot about groups of men and women but not necessarily that much about any individual man or woman. To appreciate the difference between groups and individuals in gender research, you have only to consider the issue of height. On average, men are taller than women; yet many women are taller than many men. The statement "Men are taller than women" means that if you take a random sample of around twenty-five men and women, the average height of the males will exceed the average height of the females, although there will be some short men and some tall women in the sample. This book discusses differences between men and women in the subtle ways we cope with shame and fear, allowing that there are many individual exceptions to the truths that apply to either group. We do not wish to fit any individual man or woman into one emotional category or another. We hope to shed new light on some important problems that affect most relationships and to offer a formula for overcoming those problems.

No Social Policy, Equity, Intelligence, or Aptitude Implications!

We absolutely do not believe that anything in this book has social policy implications about things like equal pay for equal work or equality of intelligence, aptitude, or opportunity. Our fervent belief is that men and women are endowed equally with intellectual gifts and aptitudes, and are equally entitled to respect and value. We just as fervently hope that the insights in this book will help us respect and value one another with greater appreciation of our individuality and connectedness, and of how we are alike, how we are different, and how we need to feel part of one another.

introduction

It's _Not_ About Communication

Let's begin by asking a question of our women readers. If you were to say to the man in your life, "Honey, we need to talk about our relationship," what do you think would happen?

If he would answer this question with something like "I thought you'd never ask!" or "I've been dying to share my feelings about our life together, and I _especially_ want to hear how you feel about us and what you want for us," then neither of you needs to read this book. _Most_ women would expect their men would get distracted, defensive, irritated, or fidgety, or roll their eyes or shut down completely; and most men would feel like they were being punished for a crime they didn't commit. Undoubtedly you've had the conversations we are talking about. She knows her lines, he knows his, and it always ends up worse than it started. No wonder the five words a man dreads most are "Honey, we need to talk."

We make it a point to ask the women in our workshops and therapy how making men talk about the relationship has worked in the past. Most say something like "It didn't work, because he can't communicate. He gets angry, defensive, or impatient. He's just not interested." Well, it turns out that when it comes to "talking about the relationship," men know something that most women don't. Research and our combined fifty-plus years of clinical experience show repeatedly that, despite your best intentions, talking about your relationship has more of a chance of making it *worse* than making it better. And it has nothing to do with your partner's lack of interest or "poor communication skills."

Women want to talk about the relationship because they're upset and want to feel better. Men *don't* want to talk because talking *won't* make them feel better. In fact, it will make them feel worse! So whether she forces him to talk or not, they both end up feeling disappointed and disconnected. **This loneliness of disconnection lies at the heart of every argument or cold silence, fueling your disappointment or resentment.** It also leads to the distance that can ultimately tear your relationship apart.

We believe the chronic stress of disconnection, which eventually afflicts most unions between men and women, stems from a slight difference in the way the sexes experience fear and shame, a difference that is observable shortly after birth. This subtle difference is inherent in the question "Do we talk about the relationship or not?" The real reason the woman wants to talk about it—beneath the resentment and frustration—is that disconnection makes her feel anxious and, on a deeper level, isolated and afraid. The real reason the man *doesn't* want to talk about the relationship is that her dissatisfaction with him makes him feel like a failure. On a deeper level, he feels ashamed. His shame is too great to allow him to understand her fear, and her fear keeps her from seeing his shame. When they try to alleviate their feelings of vulnerability in opposite ways—by talking and not talking—all they end up sharing are disappointment and heartache.

Your relationship can fail with neither of you doing anything wrong, if you do not understand the extent to which fear and shame drive your disconnection from each other. Understanding each other's core vulnerabilities and learning how to manage them will give you a new perspective on your relationship—a *dual perspective* based on both points of view—that leads to compassionate connection and love beyond words. Part I of this book will show how fear and shame have kept you both from getting what you most want out of your lives together. Part II will show you how to use your fear and shame to love each other more deeply than ever before, without asking your partner to make even *one* change. And you can do all this in just four and three-quarter minutes per day, without ever talking about your relationship! You'll be able to do it because you both *want* it.

He Wants a Close and Loving Relationship, Too

Believe it or not, research and clinical experience show that the majority of men, including those who ignore or take their partners for granted, want a closer and deeper emotional connection *just as much as women do.* For the most part, men regard their partners as their best friends, closest confidantes, and the most important people in their lives. And despite stereotypes about roving eyes and midlife crises, most men are satisfied with their partners' appearances. In fact, the majority do not want the women in their lives to change in *any* significant way.

Research and clinical experience also tell us that marriage and committed love relationships are more important to the health and well-being of men than women. Divorced men do not work as well or live as long or "survive" with anything like the quality of life enjoyed by married men. They are at considerably higher risk of alcoholism, suicide, physical and mental illness, unemployment, and car crashes or other accidents. They lose contact with friends, stop going to church or social groups, and eventually isolate themselves completely, except for whatever company they can find in a bar. In short, they lose meaning and purpose. *Without a partner, men just go through the motions of living.*

If the research is right—and our clinical experience tells us that it is dead right—men and women clearly *want* the same closeness and connection from a relationship. So why do most of us end up like Marlene and Mark?

Marlene feels emotionally disconnected from her husband. She's not quite sure when it happened, but it feels like a chilly wall has risen between them. At first it was a quiet resentment, then frequent irritability, and lately they've begun fighting. The very things they used to love about each other they now criticize. Before they got married, Marlene bragged to all her friends how she could *relax* with Mark and his "wonderfully mellow" personality. But she wants him to "get up and *do* something now and then!" Mark used to love her energy and friendliness. Now he complains about her "bouncing off the damn walls" and "giving so much to other people that there's no time left for me."

It's true—she has been doing a lot more with her girlfriends, and even when she's home, she talks to them quite a bit on the phone. But when she does try to make time for Mark, he's always distracted. He's involved with the computer or his hand is welded to the remote control or he just doesn't want to talk. She feels stupid sitting next to him in silence when she could be talking to her girlfriends, who at least care about what she has to say.

Marlene gets really sad when she remembers how hopeful she was just last week. She couldn't wait to tell Mark about the new relationship book her girlfriend gave her. It was *guaranteed* to sharpen their communication skills, clarify their expectations, and show them how to meet each other's needs. Well, it took Mark less than a minute to call it "more stupid woman talk, silly and self-centered." He shook his head at every tip she read to him, finally cutting her off in mid-sentence.

"No matter what they say about *our* needs, it always ends up being about *your* needs. Those books all tell you the same thing—to have a good relationship the man has to become a *woman*." She started to object, but he stormed out of the room with the final word on the matter: "That crap's just not me."

Last month she got him to try some "intimacy exercises" she found in a magazine. But he soon lost interest and just went through the motions, which only made her feel worse. Just three months ago he seemed to cooperate with a "rekindling romance" program she saw on *Oprah*, but he ended up sabotaging all the parts that didn't have to do with sex. Last year, after months of resisting, she *finally* got him to go to marriage counseling. But as soon as the first session was over, he told her it would be his last.

"Well, I called that right," he said. "I knew that I'd be blamed for everything."

He *did* agree to a weekend seminar on marriage enrichment and actually seemed to like it. For a week or so afterward, they felt much closer. He even became a good listener. Then one day she asked him to take the kids to his mother's, so they could have a nice romantic dinner that night. Out of nowhere, he exploded about her "constant demands," after he had "paid his damn dues" by going to the seminar.

"I can't be like that *all* the time!" he complained.

"You don't really care about me," she accused. "You just throw me a few crumbs now and then!"

"Nobody could make you happy," he countered. "You're never satisfied!"

Millions of couples suffer the same confusion and pain as Marlene and Mark. They usually blame it on each other, but sometimes they attribute their hurt to money, the kids, in-laws, problems at work, or just "a bad day." There's no doubt that they argue frequently about these things, but they are by no means the *source* of their hurt and disconnection. Furthermore, they will not correct the causes of their pain through sharpening their communication skills or by "talking about their relationship."

It's About Connection

The male-female disconnection is the biggest single factor in the soaring divorce rate. Some 80 percent of divorcees say they "grew apart." This is so tragic because it's so unnecessary. Marlene doesn't want another *girlfriend;* she wants a deeper connection with her *husband.* Yet her female-oriented attempts to get what they both want would fail even if Mark were less resistant. That's because their problem is not about "communication." It's about disconnection. **They are not disconnected because they have poor communication; they have poor communication because they are disconnected.** In the beginning of the relationship, when they felt connected, they communicated just fine. They talked for hours on end. When Marlene exposed vulnerable feelings to Mark, he responded with protectiveness and support. She fell in love because she felt emotionally connected to him, and her belief that he would be there for her quelled all her fears. Mark also fell in love because he felt emotionally connected to Marlene. She made him feel important and successful as a lover, protector, and provider, which reduced any threat of feeling inadequte. Their best chance of saving their marriage is to return to this state of mutually soothing and empowering connection.

This book will show you how to regain the kind of connection you had when you were first in love, but on a much deeper level. It will guide you and your partner to the *gut-level* emotional sensitivity that brought you together in the first place, and will enable you to forge the deeper connection for which your hearts secretly and powerfully ache—a love beyond words.

why it's been so hard to improve your relationship

how we break
the connection
Fear and Shame

things weren't always so bad for Marlene and Mark. At one time they cherished the closeness they felt—all their friends used to marvel at how close and connected they were. They can still vividly recall the good times, but instead of comforting them, these memories of the closeness they once had now fill them with sadness and a deep sense of loss. They often wonder how they got to this lonely state. Their story is all the more sad because it is so common.

Marlene and Mark arrived at their chronic state of disconnection without either of them doing anything wrong. Marlene has never grasped that Mark, like most men, has a heightened sensitivity to feeling shame and inadequacy. (How could she? His impulse when he feels shame is to *hide,* so he can't tell her about it. Instead, he disguises it with annoyance, impatience, or anger.) She does not understand that each time she tries to make improvements in their relationship, the overriding message Mark hears is that he is not meeting her expectations—he's *failing* her—which sends him into the pain of his own inadequacy. While trying to ward off feeling like a failure, Mark is no longer sensitive to Marlene's fear of being isolated and shut out. In the beginning of their relationship, he sensed her need for connection and wouldn't have dreamed of shutting her out. But now he has no idea that each time he rejects her overtures or raises his voice in anger—

purely to protect himself—he's pushing her further away and deeper into the pain of isolation.

It's so easy for couples to slip into this pattern, because the different vulnerabilities that so greatly influence the way men and women interact with each other are virtually *invisible*. In the beginning of the relationship, the falling-in-love chemicals our brains secrete make it easy to focus on each other's more subtle emotions. But once the effects of those chemicals wear off—within three to nine months—we need to make a more conscious effort to protect each other's vulnerabilities. To do this, we first need to understand the different vulnerabilities of men and women and how we manage them in our relationships.

How We're Different: Fear and Pain

The differences that underlie male and female vulnerabilities are biological and present at birth. Baby girls, from day one, are more sensitive to isolation and lack of contact. No doubt this sensitivity evolved as an important survival skill designed to keep the female in contact not only with her offspring but also with others in the group who would offer her protection. In the days of roaming predators, the only hope of survival was to help one another ward off an enemy. A woman or child left alone was sure prey. So over the millennia, females developed a kind of internal GPS that keeps them aware of closeness and distance in all their relationships. When a woman feels close, she can relax; when she feels distant, she gets anxious. This is why a baby girl can hold your gaze for a long period of time. She is comforted by the closeness the eye-to-eye contact provides. It also explains why, left alone for the same period of time, a girl baby will fuss and complain before a boy baby. This heightened sensitivity to isolation makes females react strongly to another person's anger, withdrawal, silence, or other sign of unavailability. It is more frightening to her to be out of contact than it is for a male. This is not to say that males prefer isolation or distance; it's just that females feel more *discomfort* when they are not in contact.

Men have a hard time understanding a woman's fear and the pain associated with it. One reason is that a woman's fear provokes shame in a man: "You *shouldn't* be afraid with me as your protector!" This is why he gets angry when she gets anxious or upset. But there's another reason men just don't get women's fear. They don't know what it *feels* like. Research shows the single biggest sex difference in emotions is in the frequency and intensity of fear—how often you get afraid and how afraid you get. Girls and women both experience and express far more fear, as measured in social contexts and in laboratory experiments that induce fear. Newborn girls are more easily frightened than boys. Girls and women are more likely to feel fear in response to loud noises and sudden changes in the environment. They have more anxiety and worry a lot more than boys and men. Women have a markedly higher fear of crime, even though they are far less often the victims of it. They are more likely to think about the harmful consequences of their behavior, which helps them avoid most risky behavior. They suffer more phobias and greatly exceed men in fear of medical and dental care. The fact that they *go* to doctors and dentists more often may be a tribute to their courage (ability to overcome fear) or a result of their general sensitivity to anxiety and worry, which could make them fear the consequences of not going even more.

Another reason that females have more fear of harm may be that they feel more pain. The scientific data suggest that women suffer quite a bit more physical pain than males, not counting childbirth. As early as two weeks old, girls cry louder and more vigorously than boys in response to mild pain stimulus. The higher anxiety levels of females only ratchet up their sensitivity to pain. Around 90 percent of chronic pain disorders afflict women. Men have a hard time empathizing with the pain and fear of their wives, both because they're conditioned from toddlerhood to suck it up, and because it doesn't hurt *them* as much!

How We're Different: Hyperarousal and Shame

Although boy babies feel less fear and pain than girls, they have a heightened sensitivity to any type of abrupt stimulation, which gives them a propensity for hyperarousal, that is, hair-trigger reactions. Male infants startle five times more often than female infants and are provoked by a much lower stimulus—a loud stomach gurgle will do it. (You can observe this difference if you visit a neonatal nursery in a hospital.) A male's hair-trigger propensity for hyperarousal has a distinct survival advantage. Due to his greater strength and muscle mass, the male is better equipped than the female to fight off predators. Since the primary predators of early humans stalked and attacked stealthily, males needed to respond with fight-or-flight behavior in a fraction of a second.

Because of their high sensitivity to arousal, newborn boys have to guard against the discomfort of *overstimulation*. This is why boy babies have to take eye contact and other intimate contact in small doses. If you have a boy and a girl, you may have noticed this difference. Your baby girl was able to hold eye contact almost as soon as you brought her home from the hospital. You could gaze into her big eyes (she widens them to draw in your gaze) for hours on end. But your little boy was less likely to hold that kind of eye contact before six to nine months of age, if at all. When you looked deeply into his eyes, he probably looked down, then back at your eyes, then up, then back at your eyes, then down the other side, then back at your eyes, then up the other side, then back at your eyes. He was *interested* in you—or he wouldn't have kept looking back—and he certainly wasn't afraid of you. His intermittent attention was his way of staying in contact with you without becoming overwhelmed. It's important to note that this is a function of his sensitivity to arousal, not his ability to focus, as many parents mistakenly infer. Boy babies can focus on you if you do not look directly into their eyes, and they have no trouble focusing on inanimate objects.

When it comes to relationships, women often mistake this guarded response, which many males retain throughout life, for lack of interest or even loss of love. Most of the time, he hasn't lost interest; he's merely trying to avoid the overwhelming discomfort of a cortisol dump that comes with hyperarousal. Cortisol is a hormone secreted during certain negative emotions. Its job is to get your attention by making you uncomfortable so that your discomfort drives you to do something to make the situation better. The pain a woman feels when her man shouts at her is caused by the sudden release of cortisol. A man feels this same discomfort when he is confronted with her unhappiness or criticism. He may look like he is avoiding her, but he is essentially trying to avoid a cortisol hangover for the next several hours.

So how does the male propensity for hyperarousal translate into hypersensitivity to shame? First of all, boys and girls both experience shame, which is a stop-and-hide response. The root meaning of the word *shame* is "to cover or conceal." When you're embarrassed you want to crawl into a hole, and a child feeling shame wants to cover his face because he can't bear to look at you. If you are playing with a boy or girl infant and you suddenly break eye contact and turn away, he or she will experience the physical displays of shame: reddened face, contorted facial expressions, writhing muscles, and other signs of more general distress, especially if he/she was *interested in* or *enjoying* the eye contact. In this way, shame is an auxiliary of interest and enjoyment—babies have to be interested in something or feel enjoyment to experience shame when it stops abruptly. (We learn to label this abrupt drop in interest or enjoyment as "rejection," which is what you feel when your interesting phone conversation with a friend is abruptly interrupted by his call-waiting.) Because little girls are more comfortable with longer periods of eye contact, caregivers tend to stay engaged and break contact with them less often, meaning little girls experience the shame response associated with abrupt disconnection far less often. On the other hand, if parents or caregivers don't understand a little boy's need for smaller doses of eye contact, they will break the intimate contact abruptly when the little boy looks away, constantly reinforcing the shame response, which is amplified by the extra kick of cortisol that the response produces. Males who experience this over and over develop a hypersensitivity to shame.

Studies show that parents gaze into the eyes of their little girls (and talk sweetly to them while doing it) 50 percent more than they look into the eyes of their little boys. With their sons they laugh and make nonverbal utterances, wave toys in front of them, tickle them, or pick them up to shake and roughhouse with them. Both kinds of play are of high quality—children and parents enjoy them immensely. But they are qualitatively different. Little boys need the intimate contact—albeit in small doses—just as much as they need the active play. Little girls need active play as much as they need intimate contact.

Intimacy is riskier for little boys when they have consistently felt shame in conjunction with it—*if I like it too much,* the boys learn, *they'll take it away, because I don't do it right.* From the very beginning, many little boys don't feel like they can measure up in intimate relationships. Little girls can hold eye contact, while little boys are easily overwhelmed and have to look away. The eye-contact gap is especially sad because eye contact is our principal source of intimacy throughout our lives. Boys and men are deprived of the very intimacy that would help them overcome their vulnerability to shame. If you have a baby boy, you must understand that he *likes* eye contact, but you have to be more patient with him and not start tickling him when he looks away from you. The best thing you can do for your infant son to help him manage shame in the future is allow him to feel the comfort of eye contact *gradually,* at *his pace.* Keep looking at him, and you should notice that he will stay focused on your eyes for longer and longer periods. Just being sensitive to the invisible differences in male and female vulnerabilities can shift your perception and deepen your connection—without talking about it.

How We Avoid Fear and Shame

Most of the time a woman's fear and a man's shame are *unconscious*—outside awareness. You can live a lifetime without ever hearing a man say, "I feel ashamed when you get scared of my driving" or a woman say, "I want that

Gucci bag to keep my fear of deprivation at bay." Instead you will see the tip-off indicators of fear and shame: resentment and anger (blaming your shame or fear on someone else); materialism (providing illusions of status for a man and security for a woman); people pleasing (doing things detrimental to the self to gain the admiration or approval of others); obsessions (thoughts you can't get out of your mind); and compulsive behavior like impulsive shopping, overeating, and binge drinking. All the above have temporary pain-relieving effects that work for both shame and fear.

It is not our innate differences in fear and shame that drive us apart; it is how we *manage* the differences. If you manage them with criticism, defensiveness, withdrawal, or blame, your relationship will *fail;* it's as simple as that. If you manage them with the inspiration to improve, appreciate, connect, or protect—as you'll learn to do in this book—your relationship will flourish. But it will take conscious attention for a while to overcome the force of habits that began forming very early in your life.

From early childhood, girls avoid fear by building alliances and forging emotional bonds—there is comfort and strength in numbers. Without thinking about it, Marlene reacted to her unconscious fear of isolation by seeking more closeness from Mark *and* her friends. This predominant female coping mechanism is called tend and befriend.* Women respond to stressful situations by protecting themselves and their young through nurturing behaviors—the *tend* part of the model—and forming alliances with others, particularly women—the *befriend* part. Women bond around helping one another through troubled times. The more they talk about their troubles, the closer they feel.

Because emotional bonds serve as a woman's primary source of comfort, it appalls women when men try to cope with stress in ways that seem to *threaten* emotional bonds, for example: distraction (work, TV, computer, hobbies); status seeking (work, sports, acquiring expensive toys); emotional shutdown (if you feel *nothing,* you won't feel inadequate); anger (if you

---

*University of California, Los Angeles, psychologist Shelley Taylor, Ph.D., along with five colleagues, developed the model.

numb the pain you won't feel it); and aggression (if you exert power and control, you won't feel the powerlessness of failure and inadequacy).

What women have an even harder time understanding is this: For the average male, relationships are *not* a reliable source of comfort. A man's greatest pain comes from shame, due to the inadequacy he feels in relationships; therefore, going to the relationship for comfort is like seeking solace from the enemy. Talking about the relationship, which is guaranteed to remind him of his inadequacy, is the *last* method he would use for comfort, in the same category as choosing a bed of nails for a good night's sleep. This is why he often goes to a *fight-or-flight* response to ease his distress and not to a heart-to-heart talk with the woman in his life. Fight or flight is the male equivalent of tend and befriend.

Consider this cliché of a relationship dispute. The woman is talking nonstop, following her man from room to room (to cut off his flight), until he can't stand it anymore and starts to fight with her. Though familiar to most couples, this scenario is not always the case. Sometimes it's the man who can't go to sleep until "we talk this out," while the woman, exhausted from her long day, tries to cover her head with the pillow to get to sleep. But we have noticed that even in this gender reversal, the fear and shame difference is secretly at work. The woman who follows her fleeing man from room to room is trying valiantly, if misguidedly, to achieve connection and allay her fear of isolation. But when the man keeps her up all night talking about "the problem," he is trying to prove that he is *right,* which reduces his experience of shame—he's trying to win the fight, not make connection.

The male fight-or-flight response is seen most commonly in acts of aggression and competitiveness. You have, no doubt, watched boys act out these behaviors in the neighborhood, on the school playground, and in your living room. To appreciate the relationship of aggression to shame, you have to understand only what these powerful emotional states do to your mind and body. With heavy doses of cortisol, shame hurts like hell and drains off all available energy—all you want to do is crawl into a hole. Its message is that something is producing rejection or failure—stop it and cover it up! Anger comes to the rescue with its analgesic and amphetamine-like effects that numb the pain and give a surge of energy. (This is why wounded animals are so ferocious and athletes can break a bone in a game and not even know it.) Anger and aggression ward off shame by numbing its pain and filling the void of energy it depletes. All you have to do to make a man verbally or physically aggressive is threaten him with shame: "You're a wimp, a loser, a dud, and you have a small penis!" As they used to say in the Westerns that men love so much, "Them's fightin' words!"

Shame is so painful to men that they will go to great lengths to avoid it. Most wives would be rich if they were paid for each time they had to remind their men to make doctor and dentist appointments. He's avoiding his dread of what Deborah Tannen calls the "one-down position" of help seeking; that is, he feels inadequate for being *in need*. (Yes, this is why he won't ask for directions.) You might think he is afraid of going to the doctor, but men don't have the luxury of feeling fear because fear triggers a *deeper* dread of failure, inadequacy, or loss of status. The experience of fear *is* failure for men—they feel like cowards or wimps, and if other men find out, they could lose status. "Death before dishonor" is not a phrase associated with women's groups. And there seems to be no culture that sends its preadolescent girls into the woods to earn their womanhood by overcoming fear.

Don't get us wrong, women dread the shame of failure, too, but shame tends to trigger their deeper fear of harm or isolation. Marlene's shame can be summed up this way: "If I fail, no one will help, love, or comfort me." But Mark is likely to feel: "If I fail, I won't be able to help, love, or comfort myself and I won't be *worthy* of your help, love, or comfort." When a woman fails at work, she wants more closeness in her relationship. When a man fails at work, he's likely to fight with his wife or withdraw from her and want to be left alone.

The biological difference between the sexes is only slight at birth and does not produce the large difference in behaviors we see in adults. Most of that comes from culture and socialization, which, from early childhood, set out strict ways to avoid shame and fear based on gender. The stereotype of toddler discipline is to invoke shame in boys—"Stop that, you bad boy!"—and fear in girls—"Stop that, you're going to get hurt!" Caregivers recognize that the mere threat of spanking controls the behavior of little girls, while boys suffer considerably more corporal punishment, demeaning discipline, and physical abuse, because fear is *not* a sufficient deterrent for them. Even little kids are aware of this difference. One study of eight-year-olds showed that both boys and girls *expected* that the boys would receive more humiliating forms of discipline than girls for the same behaviors. Children in both groups also believed that they would be disciplined differently if they were of the opposite sex. Parents recognize that the mere threat of harm controls girls, but with their boys they make the tragic mistake of *inflicting harm* to get their attention, which will only make them more aggressive or more withdrawn. If you kick a puppy, what kind of dog do you get?

Try this exercise. Take a moment to imagine a little girl crying in shame. She feels so bad that she can't even look at you; her sobbing face is buried in her hands as she quivers with the pain of rejection. Your every impulse is to take her in your arms and comfort her and forgive her for whatever she might have done. When addressing a group of people, Steven makes a point to ask the men in the audience, "When you were a young boy, what happened if you cried and showed that you were feeling bad about yourself?" Almost all say that they were teased or hurt even more: "What are you, a sissy?" or "Crybaby!" or "I'm going to give you something to really cry about!"

Little boys have as much of an instinct to cry in shame as little girls. For the most part, girls get comforted for doing it, and boys are rejected for it. To get the closeness they want, women have learned to *expose* vulnerability; men have learned to *hide* it.

To better understand our different core vulnerabilities, try this experiment. List the things that you *most* dread ever happening to you, no matter how unlikely they are.

WHAT DO YOU MOST DREAD?

Woman's List	Man's List
1.	1.
2.	2.
3.	3.
4.	4.

If you're a woman, your list probably contains items that, at least indirectly, involve the possibility of harm (being beaten or raped), isolation (loss of loved ones—no one to want or care about you), and deprivation (no food, shelter, comfort, or things that make you feel good). A man's list of the most dreadful things will have far fewer of those kinds of items. (If males had more fear, they wouldn't do so many risky and dangerous things from young boyhood through midlife crises.) The male list of dreadful things is primarily about the possibility of failure, inadequacy, or loss of status—inability to protect someone he loves, missing a promotion, getting fired, losing the respect of others. A man may *seem* to have deprivation on his list—losing his sexual prowess or his house, car, season tickets to the NFL—but the underlying dread is that the loss of these things will mean *failure* and loss of *status,* not deprivation. A woman will think of what life would be like without certain things; a man will think of how he couldn't look other people in the eye if he lost those things.

Here's another example. Men and women fear homelessness equally but in different ways. Women cite harm, isolation, and deprivation as their primary fears about living on the street—"Someone would hurt me," "No would care about me," and "I'd freeze, starve, and couldn't bathe." Men claim that what they could least tolerate about having to live on the street is being seen as a *failure.* "I couldn't hold my head up" is a common male response. Getting beaten up or feeling isolated doesn't even occur to many men until they hear a woman mention them, and then they'll say, "Oh, well, that wouldn't be good either."

A dire example of our different vulnerabilities is seen in how men and women commit suicide. Thousands of men took their lives after the stock market crash of 1929, but only a handful of women followed suit, even though they lost just as much money and status as their husbands. The few women who did were widowed—isolated and abandoned—by husbands who could not see beyond their own sense of failure, inadequacy, and loss of status. Despairing men tend to use suicide to escape failure at work, which stimulates the deeper shame of inadequacy as a provider and protector, while desperate women try to escape isolation. A woman might think of suicide if she feels that *no one loves her;* a man will do it if he feels that he *deserves* no one's love, because he's a failure.

The sex difference in vulnerability to fear and shame is not unique to humans; it can be observed in most species of social animals. The females are more fearful—even when they are the primary hunters—and the males are more status oriented. Female fear stimulates protective aggression in the males of most species of social animals. Due to their keener sense of hearing and smell, the females of the pack serve as its *alarm system*. When a female hears something in the middle of the night, the males wake up aggressive and form a perimeter around the females, who hide with the young. The males have no direct sense of invaders; they are merely reacting to the fear of the females. This same scenario plays out in most human families. The woman hears something in the middle of the night that frightens her. She pokes at her sleeping husband.

"Go see what that is!" she whispers.

Half asleep and without his glasses, he stumbles down the stairs with a baseball bat, while she checks on the kids and waits there for his all-clear announcement.

Are We Different in the Way We Love or in the Ways We Avoid Shame and Fear?

You may have heard that research shows a sex difference in the prosocial emotions—in general, women are more loving, compassionate, and caring. We believe that this *seeming* difference is due to the differences in our vulnerabilities rather than in the positive emotions themselves. It is riskier for women *not* to invest in love, compassion, and nurturance, because they will be more vulnerable to fear of harm, isolation, and deprivation if they don't. And it is riskier for men to invest too much in love, compassion, and nurturance, as that will make them more vulnerable to feeling like *failures* as lovers, providers, protectors, and parents. When men have no choice in the matter, for example when they are single parents, they abandon their shame-avoidant habits and become more loving, compassionate, and nurturing. Now here's the really good news for all of us. **Women, the men in your life will definitely be more loving, compassionate, and nurturing if you can understand and accept their vulnerability to shame and *reduce the ways you trigger it.***

How Fear and Shame Bring Us Together: We Soothe Each Other

Think back to the beginning of your relationship.

How many women would fall in love with a man who made it clear that he would need to approve any money she spent on herself? Would he have seemed so wonderful had he told you that after you were married he expected to go out with the guys every night, whether you were lonely or not, or that he approved of his father smacking his mother around now and then? A big reason you fell in love is that you believed on some deep level that he would be generous—within your financial means at least—attentive, and good company and that he wouldn't dream of hurting your feelings or your body.

How many men would fall in love with a woman who thought he was a loser, a lousy lay, or a wimp? A man needs to believe that his partner will be pleased with his success, be thrilled by his lovemaking, and feel safe and secure with him.

That's how it is for most couples. He soothes her anxiety and she soothes his shame simultaneously, by making each other feel important and valuable. This mutual compassion and caring are the basis of your connection.

How They Tear Us Apart:
Her Anxiety Causes His Shame
and His Shame Causes Her Anxiety

By the end of the first year of marriage Mark began to hear Marlene's perfectly reasonable requests for more closeness as *The way you love isn't good enough.* This sent him into shame-avoidant behavior—distraction, stonewalling (the cold shoulder), control, criticism, or yelling. Of course, such behavior only *increased* Marlene's fear of harm, isolation, and deprivation. This pattern is so common that you probably know few couples who haven't had the following experience while driving. The female passenger is frightened by a sudden noise or something she sees on the road. Her man interprets her involuntary reaction as an assault on his charioteering. He gets angry and drives more aggressively, making her more afraid. They argue, each feeling that the other is insensitive, inconsiderate, and immature. Similarly, many guys are at least a little insulted by the subtle anxiety of their wives as they walk together through a darkened parking garage at night if they see the fear as an indictment of their adequacy as protectors. "What are you worried about? I'm here to watch out for you!" Over time they begin to shut out their wives' anxiety to protect themselves from their shame. As a result, both feel more isolated.

Here's another reason we have a hard time being sensitive to the emotional vulnerabilities of the opposite sex. Researchers have noted that gender socialization promotes *humility* in females—you can't build alliances if you pretend to be *better* than potential allies. This tends to make women less patient with male shame-avoidant behaviors that seem *prideful*. "Just ask your brother for the loan," Marlene says to Mark. "The worst he can do is say no!" She sees his drive to avoid shame as something worse than male pride. It's *childish* and *immature,* or worse: *You don't care enough about me to swallow your stupid pride.*

At the same time it promotes humility in girls, socialization lauds *courage* in boys. This makes them less patient with female fear, which, to them, smacks of cowardice or lack of discipline. "Just stop *thinking* so much and *do* it," Mark has often told his wife. "You'll never get anywhere if you worry about every little thing that might go wrong."

Women build alliances with other women by doing what they learned in early childhood: *exposing* vulnerability. Marlene doesn't have to mention to her girlfriends that she feels sad, unhappy, lonely, or isolated. They *infer* it from her body language or tone of voice, just as she can tell if something is wrong with them. As soon as one woman senses a friend in emotional need, they become more interested and emotionally invested in each other. But what do you think happens when Marlene tells Mark that she feels bad? (She has to *tell* him—his defense against feeling failure and inadequacy has blinded him to her emotional world by this time.) You guessed it—once she forces him to face her vulnerability, he feels *inadequate* as a protector. He responds with typical shame-avoidant behavior: impatience, distractedness, defensiveness, resentment, anger, criticism, or "advice" that sounds an awful lot like telling her what to do.

After a while, a woman will stop exposing vulnerability to the man in her life and turn more to friends, allowing the emotional void in their relationship to fill with resentment. Marlene doesn't know it, but she already has one foot out the door. The probable catalyst for their breakup will be one of the following. Marlene becomes ill or depressed or loses a loved one. Feeling inadequate to help her, Mark withdraws emotionally yet again, leaving her to face her ordeal completely alone. When she recovers, she will see no need for such an unreliable alliance and leave him, thinking that they have grown apart. The other likely breakup scenario has one or both of them starting an affair, Marlene to ease her sense of isolation and Mark to prove his adequacy. *Fortunately, a breakup can easily be avoided by paying attention to each other's innate vulnerability.*

The Good, the Bad, and the Ugly of Fear and Shame Avoidance

Fear and shame are not bad things. For example, fear keeps us safe while crossing the street by making us pay attention. It also binds us together in social units, nations, communities, families, and friends, all of which lower anxiety and protect us from harm and isolation. Shame keeps us moral, humane, and true to our deepest values. A person who feels no shame is as dangerous as he is unlovable.

Aristotle said that the only virtue is **moderation,** and he couldn't have been more right when it comes to fear and shame. Moderating our primary vulnerabilities is a good thing. We're likely to have a better time at the party if we don't think about the possibility of an earthquake leveling the building or suspect that an ex-lover might have spread stories about premature ejaculation. A moderate fear of deprivation can help us enjoy shopping, and a moderate dread of shame can make us study hard for a test. But an excess of fear can make us try to avoid deprivation by overshopping, overeating, hoarding, shoplifting, or stealing. Too much fear of isolation can make us cling to others, people please, oversacrifice, tolerate bad or abusive behavior, and lose a sense of who we are as individuals. Trying too much to quell fear of harm can inhibit growth, creativity, ambition, and goal setting, and make us too conservative, too timid, and too nervous.

You probably know people who demand things like jewelry, expensive clothing, or exotic vacations to compensate for their partners' withdrawal or distraction. We've had many clients who have said things like "Well, at least I'll get a new piece of jewelry out of it." Don't judge them too harshly for their materialism. They are just trying to allay their fear of isolation (if he spends a lot he must be committed to me) and deprivation (if I have more, I won't feel deprived). It doesn't work, of course. On a deeper emotional level, it feels like the only real protection from harm and isolation is intimate connection.

You may be surprised to know that fear avoidance keeps many women in abusive relationships. You would think the instinct to avoid fear would drive them away from guys who make them live in fear. There are two important reasons it does not. One is that the risk of greater harm increases sharply when a woman leaves an abusive man. They are often threatened with injury or death if they dare to leave. The other reason may shock you. Most of the hundreds of battered women we have worked with have said that they were initially attracted to men who eventually became abusers because they made them feel *safe*. Most of them saw the aggressive and power-seeking behaviors of their fiancés as a promise of protection. Once the battering begins and her sense of reality deteriorates, she feels on some level that, as dangerous as it is in the relationship, he *does* protect her from danger outside it. Fear of isolation and deprivation also enter into it—women are more likely to leave if they have someone with resources to whom they can go.

Shame avoidance can also keep a man in a relationship with a woman who consistently criticizes and berates him—who may even strike out against him physically. You probably know relationships where you ask yourself, "Why does he put up with her?" It's so hard to understand why a wonderful, competent man tolerates her complaining and constant belittling. Here's why he does. The thought of failure of this relationship and the prospect of another man making her happy—when *he* couldn't make her happy—paralyzes him with shame and keeps him stuck in the abusive relationship.

On the darkest side, excessive shame avoidance can make us aggressive, narcissistic, and grandiose (exaggerating our looks, talents, skills, and gifts). It can also make us feel superior, contemptuous, and entitled. It can make us withdraw, shut down, and become cold and unfeeling. It can make pride more important than love and allow "humiliation" to justify murder, terrorism, and war.

Fortunately, we don't have to live on the dark side of fear and shame. In fact, we can learn to use them to improve our most important relationships and, in so doing, make the world a better place. The point we want to make here is that the fear-shame dynamic works so far outside conscious awareness that it is almost impossible to disarm it by talking about it! The connection we want most must go beyond words.

One reason that talking about your relationship has not helped is that fear and shame keep you from *hearing* each other, regardless of how much "active listening" or "mirroring" you try to do. The prerequisite for listening is feeling safe, and you cannot feel safe when the threat of fear or shame hangs over your head. The threat is so dreadful that the limbic system, the part of your brain in charge of your safety, overrides any form of rational thinking. Almost everything you hear invokes fear or shame.

Remember the famous *Far Side* cartoon of the man talking at length to his dog, Ginger? One bubble had what the man said and the other had what Ginger heard. The man said a lot, but this is all that Ginger heard:

"Blah blah **Ginger** blah blah blah blah blah blah blah blah **Ginger** blah blah blah blah blah . . ."

Unless a woman is emotionally connected to her partner, this is what he will hear when she talks to him:

"Blah, blah, blah, **failure.** Blah, blah, blah, **not good enough.** Blah, blah, blah, **can't meet my needs.** Blah, blah, blah, **bad boy.**"

Unless a man is emotionally connected to his partner in a way that promotes safety, this is what she will hear when he criticizes her, no matter how "right" he may be:

"Blah, blah, blah, **I don't love you.** Blah, blah, blah, **I won't be there for you.** Blah, blah, blah, **I might even harm you.**"

And when he ignores or stonewalls her, she hears the true sound of silence:

"——, **I don't love you.** ——, **I won't be there for you.** ——, **I might even harm you.**"

The Good News Lies Deeper

There is a very different message, resonating beyond words, that runs deeper than even the fear-shame dynamic. Though powerful and pervasive, your fear and shame are not the deepest or most important things about you. Much deeper is the compassionate, loving part of you that was so active when you were a child and when you were first in love with each other. It's still there, although it may be hidden beneath the resentment that makes you fight and the fear and shame that make you resentful. As you read the rest of Part I, know that the warm glow is still within you, waiting to ignite your spirit, which we will help it do in Part II.

two

why we fight

The Reactivity of Fear and Shame

She's so *unreasonable!*" Randy said with disgust, after describing the incident that caused Sheila to insist that he make this therapy appointment.

"I'm afraid to ask if you actually tell her she's unreasonable," Steven said.

"Of course I tell her. She has to know."

"Then she probably said something like 'You're so insensitive!' "

"Yes," he said, as if Steven had supported his point. "I try to use reason and logic, and she just gets more and more irrational." He was quite prepared to keep going, but Steven knew that would be counterproductive, so he posed the same question to Randy he'd asked the hundreds of men who had sat in the same chair and uttered the same incantation.

"How *rational* is it to keep trying an approach that always fails?"

Apart from the fact that what we really mean when we characterize someone as "unreasonable" or "irrational" is that we disagree with them, there is a lot more to what makes something reasonable than its degree of intellectual logic. A computer is logical, but how many important decisions in your life would you want a computer to make? And would you want to marry a computer, even if it looked like Brad Pitt or Nicole Kidman?

Most "Logical Disagreements" Are Really About Fear and Shame

When Randy called Sheila irrational he implied that she used only half her brain—the more intuitive and emotional right side, to be precise. It's tempting to say that when Randy made the accusation, he used only half of his brain, too—the logic-mathematical left side. It was a case of one person using half a brain to accuse another of using half a brain. But in truth they were both using only the *reactive* part of their brains. Randy wasn't just trying to illuminate facts or utter elegant logical theorems or even persuade Sheila to adopt his opinion; he was trying to *devalue* hers. His determination to undermine her perspective drove the entire line of "reasoning" that prompted him to describe his wife as "irrational." Dedication to logic does not make you attack or devalue. (That's why *Star Trek*'s Mr. Spock never got upset with those who disagreed with him.) If Randy had really wanted to just get to the facts, he wouldn't have resorted to labeling or name-calling. Devaluing is an attempt to demean others and elevate ourselves. More specifically: **We devalue those we love in an attempt to avoid our own shame or fear.**

Here's another example. Sheila says, "It's cold in here."

Randy replies, "How can you say that? It's seventy degrees!"

Randy believes he is contradicting Sheila, when, in fact, he is not addressing her point at all. They are talking about different domains of human experience. He is analyzing the room temperature, while she is reporting her sensation. Far from a logical analysis of the relationship between sensation and temperature, Randy's remark is completely *reactive;* he wasn't thinking or listening, he simply responded in a knee-jerk fashion. His reactivity was meant to devalue an opinion that he found threatening. ("If she's cold, it must be my fault; I've failed to make her happy and protect her from discomfort.") Of course, his reaction makes Sheila react. She now feels he doesn't value her, which raises her anxiety. They are both feeling devalued by the other, even though no one is trying to devalue anybody. They are trying to avoid the discomfort of their own underlying shame and fear. Of course, their self-protective feelings are *unconscious*. All they know is that they're pissed at each other.

The fact that it is seventy degrees in the room neither supports nor contradicts Sheila's sensation of being cold. Their statements provide *different* bits of information, with unique contributions to the discussion. Couples make a terrible mistake when they think that one kind of response, be it mostly logical or mostly emotional, is superior to the other. In reality, they are different dimensions, each important in its own right.

Just the Facts, Ma'am

Randy is like a lot of men who believe women can't reason as well as men. **There is *no* scientific evidence that one sex *reasons* better than the other.** There is a very slight advantage that women hold in logical-emotional *integration*. That means they can more efficiently use information processed by their emotional brains with that processed by their logical brains. Men are more likely to use one side at a time. They tend to be logical *or* emotional, while women can be both at once.

Women enjoy this mental advantage due to a combination of nature and nurture. As we have seen, many studies show that we condition little girls in a variety of ways to be more in touch with their emotions and to consider them more prominently in their decision making. We applaud Johnny for riding his bike faster than other boys because he is focused on winning. But we expect Jeannie to consider the feelings of the little girl who lags behind her. There is also evidence that women have a slightly larger corpus callosum, the region of the brain that connects the hemispheres. Though it is not known for certain, it's plausible that the extra cells in this area enable women to incorporate more right-brained input into their reasoning.

Women typically have more emotional information at their disposal than men do. While this can sometimes obscure the point at hand, it more often introduces an extra dimension that may not change the facts but will often change their meaning. For instance, winning the race will mean something different to the girl who considers the feelings of the child lagging behind her than to the boy who has no interest in how the losers might feel—he's just glad not to be one of them.

There is good news in the slight male advantage in focusing on facts relatively free of emotion, coupled with the slight female advantage in processing facts in the deeper emotional context: We make a good team. And we can stay a good team throughout marriage, as long as we don't try to change or control each other or put each other down with accusations of too little heart or too much emotion.

The real sex difference in thinking isn't that women are less rational and men less emotional. It's that men try to *ignore* some of the information provided by their emotions, in part because there is so much cultural shame attached to men expressing emotions. From an early age, being a "big boy" meant being rational, not emotional. Thus Randy deceives himself about being logical in his put-down of Sheila. His refusal to be open to the emotional content of their exchange makes Sheila anxious about their connection. Thus, the couple's disputes about things like bills and the temperature in the house are powered by her fear of deprivation and isolation and his dread of failure as a provider, not by a difference in reasoning.

The fear-shame dynamic that powers so many of our arguments forces us to make an artificial distinction between logic and emotion. The fact is that *emotions are logical.* For millennia they were the sole motivators and regulators of behavior before we developed a primitive capacity for intellectual reasoning. The neocortex—the brain's logic-rational mantel that sits like a crown over its older and more venerable motivational systems—initially developed to interpret, test, and explain emotional responses to the environment. Even in the advanced cortical development of the modern brain, the typical processing sequence still goes like this. A change in the environment triggers an emotional response. The neocortex assesses the change and decides either to temper or to enhance the emotional response.

Change in environment $\longrightarrow$ Emotional response $\longrightarrow$ Cortical interpretation and behavioral choice

Imagine you suddenly see a light from the corner of your eye while you're driving. You startle—a biological mechanism that prepares you for fight or flight. Your neocortex weighs the emotion according to two factors: your current capacity to cope and the environmental stimulus, in this case the light. If it's a car careening toward you, you veer away from it. Or if it was just a reading lamp in the SUV passing you, you refocus on the road ahead. Without the intellectual response, you would be reduced to fight-or-flight choices—you would attack the light or run away from it. Without the emotional response preparing you for action, you wouldn't act quickly enough to survive if the light turned out to be on an oncoming car.

Randy and Sheila, in reaction to each other's shame and anxiety, tried to separate reasoning from emotion as if one dimension were superior to the other—she's unreasonable, he's unfeeling. In reality, the human brain treats reasoning and emotion as different parts of the same process. To function as a whole person, we need to integrate *both* sides of the brain. Most of our fights that seem to highlight a difference in thinking between men and women are not about differences in reasoning and emotions at all—they're about the hidden reactivity to fear and shame.

Why We're So Reactive to Fear and Shame

This probably has happened to you more than a few times. You come home in a fairly decent mood and find that your partner is in a bad mood. He or she isn't doing anything big to tip you off; there's no sarcasm, cold shoulder, silent treatment, or anything like that. Still, there's something not quite right, even though you can't put your finger on it. Subtle though it may be, it's enough to make you feel like a button's been pushed in you; all of sudden your decent mood is gone and you're in a bad mood, too.

For each incident like this that you happened to notice, there were hundreds of which you were unaware. They result from an almost entirely *unconscious* process called *emotional attunement*. Our bodies—not just our brains—automatically *tune* our emotions to those of people we love. Newborns, adults, and family dogs do it. Teenagers try to *stop* doing it in preparation for leaving the pack, and they come off as sulky, moody, and disagreeable for their efforts, as do adults when they try to cut off emotional attunement.

To understand the power of emotional attunement you only have to consider its survival advantage. Sharing emotions gives us multiple eyes, ears, and noses with which to sense danger and opportunity. When one member of the tribe (pack, herd, flock, or pride) becomes aggressive, frightened, or interested, the others reflexively tune to the same emotion with more or less the same behavioral motivation.

Emotional attunement is why your choice of words has little to do with the success of your relationship, regardless of how many "communication" classes you take. Humans bonded, cooperated, and communicated by emotional attunement many thousands of years before we had verbal language. Our vocalizations then were the same as those of all social animals, serving primarily as a tuning fork to get the group reattuned to the emotion of the moment. A grunt or a shriek gets the distracted, sleeping, or daydreaming members of the group back to emotional attunement. In humans, tone of voice now serves the same purpose. Although we try to fool ourselves with words, it is body language, facial expressions, scent, and tone of voice that most influence emotional attunement. That's why we can't get away with saying one thing while our bodies say another, as in the male favorite: "Nothing's wrong, I just don't feel like talking." Guys, you might find some women who would go along with this in the face of your tense facial expressions and rigid musculature, but you'd be hard-pressed to find any who would truly buy it. Even thinking a negative thought will show up in your facial expressions and body language. This is why it feels different sitting next to someone who is angry or irritable (even if they say nothing is wrong) versus someone who is in a good place.

Although it helped us survive over the ages, emotional attunement can present problems in modern relationships, due to its negative bias. Because negative emotions are geared more to emergencies of survival, they get priority processing in the central nervous system. That was great for fighting off predators lurking near the cave entrance, but it's not so well designed for coming home from the office. If you walk in the door in a really good mood only to find your partner in a really bad mood, the attunement process will bring him up a little and take you down a *lot*. It's certainly not because either of you *wants* it that way; you are both victims of the inherent negative bias of emotional attunement. In intimate relationships even an unconscious negative emotion will stimulate a reactive response in your partner. For example, a woman's anxiety will stimulate shame in a man and a man's shame will stimulate a woman's anxiety—and the spiral can go downward from there. **This is why even unspoken anxiety in women stimulates shame in men and even unspoken shame in men stimulates anxiety in women.**

It's crucial to understand that the downward pull on your emotions is not due to the malevolent will of your partner but to the survival significance of emotional attunement. If you do not understand this process, one of you will begin to think that the other purposefully "brings you down," and start to shut out his or her emotions. The disruption of emotional attunement—for the sake of avoiding fear and shame—puts you squarely on the path to divorce. Much of the resentment that occurs in relationships is not about material unfairness; it's about the perception that your emotions are controlled, if not manipulated, by your partner—he makes you anxious, and she makes you feel like a failure.

Power Struggles

In a nutshell, power struggles happen when two people fight to protect themselves from shame and fear. She wants him to do what she wants so she doesn't have to feel anxious, and he wants her to give in so he doesn't have to feel like a failure. They try to control each other or even force the other to submit. Because human beings hate to submit, power struggles *always* result in more resentment and hostility, which only aggravate fear and shame.

Here's the form a typical power struggle takes.

She: If you do this, I will feel (calm, loved, appreciated, grateful, supported). If you *don't* do it, I will feel (anxious, sad, unloved, exploited, betrayed, angry, resentful).

He: But if I do what you want, I will feel (inadequate, sad, unloved, exploited, betrayed, angry, or resentful).

She: If you do what I want but feel *those* things, I will still feel (anxious, sad, unloved, exploited, betrayed, angry, or resentful).

He: You have no right to feel that way.

She: You have no right to say that I have no right to feel that way. If you loved me you would do it.

He: If you loved me you wouldn't ask me to do it.

We cannot emphasize too strongly that these kinds of power struggles are *not* about content—whatever it is that you want your partner to do. They are about the powerful reactivity of shame and fear. That's how you can figure out the problem in the example above without knowing what she wants him to do. All you need to know is that she wants him to prove that he loves her, so she can feel connected and thereby reduce her fear of isolation or deprivation. But the fact that she wants him to *prove* that he loves her makes him feel like a failure—if he were a good husband, he wouldn't have to prove it.

The more reactive you are to fear or shame, the more you will feel disconnected from your partner. Unfortunately, much of the reactivity you experience is connected to history—not just your history with your partner but *all* your history. Old pain can easily get stimulated by current interactions. But the good news is once you understand the nature of reactivity and its connection to fear and shame, you and your partner can quit hurting and start healing each other.

To help you get a reading on the strength of your reactivity, we have devised the following surveys. They are not a test or an assessment of any kind; they are simply a you-are-here map. Think of them as a point of departure; we'll get you to where you want to be in Part II. The first survey is for women, the second for men.

FID Index (Fear, Isolation, Deprivation)

A SURVEY FOR WOMEN

Answer "true" or "false"

1. I have been separated from someone I love at some time in my life.
2. I have experienced the death of a significant person in my life.
3. I have experienced the death of more than one important person.
4. More than one parent/grandparent died before I was twenty-one.
5. I had a close family member who died suddenly.
6. I have had periods in my life when I felt insecure.
7. I grew up with little or no contact with my biological mother.
8. I grew up with little or no contact with my biological father.
9. My parents were divorced.
10. I was separated from one or both of my parents before age eighteen.
11. I have lived with a physically or mentally ill parent.
12. I have lived with someone who was addicted to alcohol or drugs.
13. At times growing up, I felt like more of an adult than my parents.
14. I had to be responsible for myself at a very early age.
15. My parents were so busy it was hard to get their time and attention.

16. I have experienced times when food, clothing, and/or shelter were scarce.   _____

17. I grew up in poverty or limited financial security.   _____

18. I grew up feeling like I never got enough time and attention.   _____

19. More than once growing up, I didn't fit in socially.   _____

20. I have lived with a perfectionist.   _____

21. I am a perfectionist.   _____

22. I have lived with a preoccupied, depressed, or anxious person.   _____

23. I have lived in an unsafe environment or with an untrustworthy person.   _____

24. I have lived with a very controlling person.   _____

25. I have lived with someone prone to angry outbursts and/or rage.   _____

26. I have seen people I love be threatened with anger and/or criticism.   _____

27. I have lived with physical violence.   _____

28. I have seen someone I love get threatened.   _____

29. I have been betrayed by someone I love.   _____

30. I have experienced sexual abuse, directly or indirectly.   _____

31. Feeling left out is familiar to me.   _____

32. My life has had many ups and downs.   _____

33. It seems like others get more attention than I.   _____

34. I compare myself to others.   _____

35. I feel inadequate.   _____

36. I tend to question my own capability.   _____

37. I am critical of others.   _____

38. I am critical of myself.   _____

39. I never know when my mood is going to change.   _____

40. I have been told that I am reactive (people never know when I am going to be critical, angry, or anxious, or when I will threaten to leave).   _____

Total of "true" answers   _____

Circle the number of the five most significant statements to which you answered "true." Weight each on a scale of 1 to 10, with 10 representing "very significant" in terms of stress, intensity, or trauma and 1 being "not very significant" in terms of stress, intensity, or trauma. Add these scores to a total score below. (Example: If you circled number 27, "I have lived with physical violence," you would rate the trauma of that event on a scale of 1 to 10, with 10 being "very traumatic.")

1. _____
2. _____
3. _____
4. _____
5. _____

Total of 1 through 5 _____
Total of "true" answers _____
Overall total (out of a possible 90) _____

SIF Index (Shame, Inadequacy, Failure)

A SURVEY FOR MEN

Answer "true" or "false"

1. I grew up with little or no contact with my biological mother. _____
2. I grew up with little or no contact with my biological father. _____
3. My parents were divorced. _____
4. I felt responsible for another person (emotionally or physically) when I was very young. _____
5. I grew up with a significant caretaker who was unhappy. _____
6. I have seen someone I love go through a period of unhappiness. _____
7. There was a time when I wanted to protect my loved one(s) but could not. _____

8. I remember feeling powerless at a young age. _____

9. I felt I had to be strong growing up. _____

10. It was hard to measure up to expectations as I got older. _____

11. There have been times in my life when I felt I had to make up for others' inadequacies. _____

12. I have lived with a lot of criticism. _____

13. I have lived with one or more angry persons. _____

14. I had one or more family members with very high expectations of me. _____

15. There were aspects of my family I didn't want others to know about. _____

16. I have lived with a perfectionist. _____

17. I am a perfectionist. _____

18. I have been through a period of distress with my career at some time. _____

19. I have lost an important job. _____

20. I have had an abrupt change in an important job at one time. _____

21. My attitude has been cited as a problem in one or more jobs. _____

22. I have had a significant disappointment in one or more jobs. _____

23. I am underutilized in my present job. _____

24. I'd feel better if I made more money. _____

25. There are ways I'd like to help people I love, but money prevents it. _____

26. I wish I had more power and influence. _____

27. I have lived with violence in my life. _____

28. I have lived with sexual abuse, direct or indirect. _____

29. I have a problem with anger. _____

30. Other people think I have a problem with anger. _____

31. I had a parent or grandparent who was anxious or depressed. _____

32. I know I have hurt some of the important people in my life. _____

33. I have been in an unhappy relationship. _____

34. I have lived with an unhappy partner. _____

35. I have lived with a partner who had problems I could not resolve. _____

36. I feel inadequate in my relationship(s). _____

37. My partner is unhappy with me. _____

38. I just can't seem to do enough. _____

39. I am anxious/depressed or have been told I'm anxious/depressed. _____

40. At times I feel hopeless when it comes to making my partner happy. _____

Total of "true" answers _____

Circle the number of the five most significant statements to which you answered "true." Weight each on a scale of 1 to 10, with 10 representing "very significant" in terms of trauma and 1 being "not very significant" in terms of difficulty or trauma. Add these scores to a total score below. (Example: If you circled number 29, "I have a problem with anger," you would rate the significance of that statement on a scale of 1 to 10, with 10 being "very significant.")

1. _____

2. _____

3. _____

4. _____

5. _____

Total of 1 through 5 _____

Total of "true" answers _____

Overall total (out of a possible 90) _____

Understanding Your Survey Results

As stated earlier, these surveys are not assessment devices. They are not designed to label you or put you in a category. They are simply a way to provide an objective view of experiences that can influence your sensitivity to fear and shame. Look at your total score and place it within one of the following ranges:

Low	0 to 50	_____
Moderate	51 to 75	_____
High	76 to 90	_____

Girls are born with more sensitivity to isolation and fear; boys are born with more sensitivity to arousal and shame. These differences remain slight when parents are attuned to them, for the children need not develop elaborate avoidance strategies to cope with their vulnerabilities. If, however, a woman's natural fear of isolation has been stimulated over and over by experiences that include isolation, deprivation, or harm, her neural pathway leading to fear becomes more like a superhighway with all roads leading to Rome. Likewise, if a man's natural sensitivity to shame has been stimulated over and over, his neural pathway forms a rut and he develops a hair-trigger response to any issue related to failure or inadequacy. If he's been criticized over and over, he can hear criticism even in the most sincere praise. Once this rut gets that deep, it draws all thoughts into it. He may react defensively to a simple request or say no before he even thinks about what's being proposed. If a woman's natural fear of deprivation or isolation has been repeatedly stimulated, she'll become anxious around any issue related to time investment, attention, or contact. She can easily be seen as unreasonable or insatiable. Repeated experiences that evoke fear and shame reinforce the negative bias of attunement. Individuals with strong fear or shame bias have a predisposition to negativity.

Since personal objectivity is extremely difficult, surveys such as these can give you valuable information about yourself as well as your partner. When you can see yourself as others see you (especially your partner), you are well on your way to improving your relationship without talking about it.

Before we move on, if you scored high on your respective scale, here's a special note from Pat:

I grew up in an unsafe environment. (My score on the Fear, Isolation, Deprivation index is 78 out of a possible 90 points.) Needless to say, there have been many consequences of this early experience. For years, I was afraid of my own feelings, somehow believing if I let myself feel anything, I would fall into a bottomless pit and never come out. I couldn't be compassionate with others' pain because I had so much fear of my *own* pain. I avoided my feelings by blaming them on others; staying busy; denying; going numb; being confused; acting impulsively; being a Pollyanna; and rushing through life, enjoying very little. I remember feeling like I was watching my own life on a movie screen—but I wasn't in the movie. I was so out of touch with my protective sense of fear I let the wrong people in and kept the right people out. I was literally running scared. Finally, much later in life than I wish, I mustered the courage to trust a few people by letting them into my private world. I let them support me, I let them get to know me, and I started enjoying life like I do today. So I write this personal message to encourage you. Step into someone's life (feel his or her emotions), and let others step into yours. If you lived through your history, you certainly can live through any feeling that comes up connected to that history. I'm not suggesting that you have to spill your guts or even talk about your past, but simply trust that you have the inner strength to accept compassion when it comes your way.

One last note on the hyperreactive response to fear and shame: Each of us at birth is given a genetic hand of neurochemicals to help us regulate our emotions. Optimal levels of these neurochemicals enable us to manage the stress of normal life. For example, serotonin serves as a natural sedative. It calms us; quiets the mind; lowers anxiety, irritability, and anger; and inhibits rage. When your serotonin levels are normal, it's easier to control your reactivity; you can hold a positive outlook and let go of anger and negative thoughts. When serotonin levels are low, however, you are anxious and more reactive; your outlook is gloomy; you obsess about negative events; you are more prone to anger and irritability, and you can fall quickly into fear and shame. Hormones have a similar effect on your mood and ability to manage your emotions. Without estrogen, for example, a woman is hypersensitive to insult; she cries more often, lacks a zest for life, and has a general feeling of dissatisfaction. Fortunately, it's easy to test these levels. A visit to your physician can help you obtain the information that you need and the most helpful treatment approach for you. There are so many resources available today, love beyond words is an option for all of us.

How Do You *Want* to Respond?

While attunement is an unconscious process that happens automatically, how we respond is completely within our control—all it takes is conscious effort. Without conscious effort, attunement and its negative bias are unlikely to make you happy, due in large part to the reactivity of fear and shame. Attunement can even make you a "reactaholic," helplessly addicted to its negative bias. For example, Sheila reacts to Randy's sulking by trying to get him to talk. Specifically, she points out how immature his sulking is, which he hears as yet another example of how he fails her as a husband. Randy reacts to Sheila's nagging by stonewalling. This time Sheila tires quickly of hitting her head against the stone wall (she's done it all night in the past), and they settle into a silent standoff that lasts for a couple of hours. By bedtime, Randy is tired of sulking and tries to make connection by playing with her beloved little dog in front of her. But Sheila, still hurt by the stonewalling, reacts to his olive branch by pouting—she wants an apology, which at the moment feels humiliating to him. He reacts to her pouting with his oft-repeated accusation that nothing pleases her. She reacts to that by calling him cold and insensitive and accuses him of just trying to set her up to have sex after not speaking to her all night. The saddest part of this situation is that neither of them *wants* to respond in this way; they both want to feel more connected. But the fear-shame dynamic, fueled by reactivity, blocks them at every turn.

In Part II, we'll show you in step-by-step detail how to respond to each other's fear and shame in the way you both really want, with compassion and protection. You will be surprised at how easy it will be, with the right skills, to convert the reactivity of fear and shame into a deeper connection that goes beyond words.

three

the silent male

What He's Thinking and Feeling

every marriage therapist has heard it a thousand times. The tearful wife says softly, "I don't think he really loves me anymore," and the husband's jaw drops in astonishment.

"What do you mean I don't love you, I go to work every day!" he protests.

"You would do that *anyway,*" she says scornfully.

He sighs in frustration like he's ready to throw in the towel. She definitely holds the trump card here; he *would* still go to work every day if she left. Typically at this point in the session, he grows silent and would, if we let him, sulk, stonewall, and eventually start blaming her. We don't let him because, after working with thousands of men over many years, we finally understand what they would *like* to reply if they could only formulate the words: "It's true; I would go to work every day if you left me, but it wouldn't *mean* the same."

Men have a hard time giving the reasons they value their wives, because their wives are the reason they value everything else. Women make it possible for their men to find enjoyment in watching sports, cooking, tinkering with the car, and hanging out with friends—plus, she gives meaning to his going to work every day. We can say with confidence to the majority of women reading this book that, without you, he would just go through the motions of life. Be very clear about this: In all likelihood, *you provide the meaning of his life.*

The Toll of Divorce on Men

The devastating effects of divorce on a man present a strong argument for the fact that his partner provides the meaning of his life. In terms of physical and mental health, as well as job performance and concentration, divorce is more devastating for men than for women (just think of the emotional well-being of your male friends whose wives have left them). The following are a few of the effects of divorce on the health, well-being, safety, and job performance of men:

- High error rates
- Impaired problem solving
- Narrow and rigid focus (can't see other perspectives)
- Lowered creativity
- High distractibility
- Heavy foot on the gas while driving
- Hair-trigger reactivity
- Anxiety, worry, depression
- Resentment, anger, aggression
- Alcoholism
- Poor eating habits
- Isolation
- Shortened life span
- Suicide

Make no mistake, women suffer after divorce, too, but in general the benefits of marriage and the psychological harm of divorce skew considerably toward men. This is partly because women maintain and nurture the family's social support structure. They remember people's birthdays and anniversaries, which couples like which kinds of movies, and whose turn it is to go where for dinner. When women leave the marriage, they take that support network with them, while their abandoned men wonder why no one calls. (Guys, you have to call *them* if you want *them* to call you.) Divorced women rarely face the same kind of emotional isolation as divorced men. They are less likely to develop mental health problems, alcoholism, and suicidal tendencies, and are extremely unlikely to engage in high-risk behaviors like speeding and playing with guns. By almost every measure, marriage is more essential to men than to women.

So Why Doesn't He Show It?

Because he's *ashamed*. Many men invest little positive emotion in their relationships for one single reason—to reduce the pain of failure that seems inevitable. Deep in their hearts, so many of the men we have seen in therapy expect that one day their complaining partners will get fed up with their inadequacies and leave them all alone. It may not seem to the women in their lives that they feel inadequate about relationships, because they blame all the problems on their wives: "You want too much" or "You don't know what you want" or "Nothing's good enough for you" or "*Nobody* could make you happy." He may even sound convinced, but such statements always cover up a deep sense of inadequacy. Men feel powerless about relationships. Whether they're college professors or truck drivers, dentists or mailmen, psychologists or farmers, they're pretty much in the same sorry boat when it comes to making relationships work; and they'd be the first to admit it, if their wives didn't beat them to it.

It's not entirely men's fault that they have trouble with relationship skills. It's not the specialty of the male brain. They *can* do it, it just takes more effort. For example, the ability to interpret emotion and comprehend nonverbal messages is housed in the right brain's limbic area where the female brain excels. Even in adulthood it's harder for men to interpret subtle emotions, putting them at a distinct disadvantage in male-female relationships. On the other hand, the right frontal lobe, which holds innate mechanical and spatial acuity, is much larger in males, giving them a distinct advantage with mechanical and technical tasks.

We remember one college professor complaining that, despite restricting her young son's access to TV and her careful purchase of only educational and gender-neutral toys, he still made a gun out of his breakfast toast. Do these brain differences mean that men are destined to be closer to machines and women destined to be clueless about mechanics? Absolutely not! Now, more than ever, females are excelling in formerly male-dominated fields, while a growing number of men are entering fields that focus on nurturing, such as nursing and health care. More are choosing to be stay-at-home husbands. (A recent study of the top ten Fortune 500 female CEOs found that six of the ten had stay-at-home husbands.) More men are more involved with their children, and increasing numbers are taking on the role of single parents.

Men and women who break stereotypes, however, do have to overcome some of their early learning. Like all social mammals, human children learn by a process called modeling. They closely *watch* and mimic the behavior of the same-sex parent. (You may have noticed that they don't listen much to what you say; they learn by watching you.) Little girls watch their mothers display all kinds of relationship skills with friends, family, and strangers in the grocery store. Boys, on the other hand, watch their fathers, who still spend the majority of their time working outside the home or interacting with inanimate objects. But the gap in relationship skills begins even earlier than when parental and social modeling kicks in. It begins with parent-infant bonding. For the most part, it's easier to bond with little girls than with little boys (remember the discussion of eye-contact differences between boys and girls in Chapter 1). When it comes to toddlers, parents sit girls on their laps, look into their eyes, and talk to them about pleasant feelings. ("You're so sweet and adorable." "You make me so happy.") With their little boys, parents tend to get on the floor and play with cars, trucks, and action figures. Interestingly, one study of monkeys showed that the young females chose toys like dolls and baby carriages to play with, while the males chose trucks, balls, and guns.

In preschool, where the pressures of socialization begin to escalate, boys play action-oriented and more organized types of games, while girls practice relationship skills—pretending to be mommies, wives, and best girlfriends. In school, boys talk only to other boys about *doing* things, *anything* that excludes girls. On the other hand, girls talk only to girls, mostly about how they should and should not relate to certain other girls, adults, pets, plants, and even boys. By the time they're adolescents, boys think of relationships as being no more complicated than having sex, while teen girls fantasize about the details of dating, engagement, marriage, motherhood, and career, as well as sex.

All of this means that, in general, it's easier to form a close connection with a girl. She follows you around, looking for it. You can certainly form a close attachment with a boy and, thankfully, most parents are able to do it. But it takes more work. You have to *find* him to do it. So girls, watching their mothers, learn that they have to make a special effort to bond with males, while boys learn that they don't have to do *anything* because the females will do all the relationship work for them. It's little wonder that so many men feel shocked and bewildered when their wives start making emotional demands on them after marriage.

Where Can Shocked and Bewildered Males Turn for Help?

Most relationship books and marriage-enrichment programs are designed to appeal to the women who buy or attend more than 90 percent of them. From the male perspective, these books and programs seem to imply that to have a strong relationship you have to learn to relate to your wife in the way that women like to relate to one another. That leaves men the choice, as many of our clients have put it, of becoming "like a woman" or growing more emotionally isolated in marriage. Almost all choose the latter, until their wives get fed up and threaten to leave them. Such threats, whether implied or explicit, might make them try to be more like women for a little while, as Mark did in response to Marlene's demands in Chapter 1, but their efforts are almost certain to lead to disappointment for both partners.

What Do Men Want?

Men see relationship and marriage more as a *place to relax* than a dynamic interaction. It's a secure place to get their batteries recharged before the world takes another whack at them. Ideally, it's an unchallenging place, where he can kick back, unwind, and be himself without having to play roles or manage pretenses or do things he doesn't want to do. What *makes* it relaxing is the comfort of having his partner in the room or at least in the next room. For men, a relationship is a *secure base,* as long as his partner is around or nearby.

Women also want to feel secure enough to relax in their relationships, but for them, the security comes from *interactions* with their men. They want to feel emotionally connected so they *can* relax. If she doesn't feel connected, she starts to feel anxious and alone. So both men and women want to have their relationship be a secure a base, but "security" feels different for each. **He thinks he's honoring the relationship because he can relax with her in the room (or the next room), and she thinks he's failing the relationship because he's not interacting with her.** Don't worry, Part II will show you how to reconcile these differences without anyone having to change who they are. We just want to make the point here that the security both parties want from the relationship has a different meaning for each.

Male Emotions

Although men can seem cold and indifferent, they are actually a lot more susceptible to feeling overwhelmed by their emotions. Most of their anger, emotional shutdown, and seemingly cold intellectual analysis is a defense against feeling overwhelmed and out of control. Remember, a male feels an enormous amount of physical and psychological discomfort when he experiences the jolt of hyperarousal—and he's always guarding against it. When a woman asks him to "get in touch with his feelings," it's like asking him to get in touch with a red-hot horseshoe. He was conditioned early in life to hide his emotions, not necessarily to regulate them.

Here is the key thing to remember about a man's emotions: He has to ease into them *gradually,* not abruptly. He has to make sure it is safe to go in the water. Psychologist John Gottman's research allows him to predict divorce with over 90 percent accuracy. He has found the number one thing women do to men that leads to divorce is what he calls "harsh start-up," which is a high-arousal beginning to a conversation, something like "I'm tired of telling you this" or "Why can't you ever listen to me?" It doesn't have to be loud; it can be very soft—"Honey, we need to talk." It doesn't have to be verbal; it can be a door slammed, a chair scraped along the floor, or a dish banged on the table. The guy gets flooded by the abruptness, and she's lost him. (If you're wondering about the number one thing that men do to women that predicts divorce, it's stonewalling, which is often a response to harsh start-up—or a preemptive defense against it. Conversely, harsh start-up is often an attempt to break through stonewalling.) The male sensitivity to all things abrupt, as we saw in Chapter 1, begins at birth. By the time he's an adult, his emotions are like an invisible clitoris; you should not be too direct too quickly.

Intimate talk, for instance, causes higher physiological arousal in men— with greater central nervous system activity, more blood flow to the muscles, and a lot more impulsivity—than women experience. (When a man *feels* something he *has* to *do* something.) Sitting still, looking into each other's eyes, and talking about emotions may be comforting to women (if he can make it sound sincere) but *physically uncomfortable* for men. This accounts for the squirm factor that many men are likely to display when their partners sit them down, look into their eyes, and talk about emotions. (Remember how your little boys fidgeted when you looked into their eyes, especially if you were telling them what they did wrong?) It's no accident that women report on surveys that they have the best talks with their partners under three conditions: on the phone (they don't see him piddling around to reduce his excess arousal) and while walking or driving, because he's *doing* something and not looking directly at her. On top of all this, when she tries talking to him about emotional issues, his inability to give her what she wants with any consistency makes him feel more inadequate and triggers more pouting, yelling, or stonewalling.

Recall Marlene and Mark from Chapter 1. She valiantly tried in a variety of ways to improve their relationship, but all she got in return were a few short-term changes, a lot of resistance, and outright rejection. Nothing she tried worked—but not for lack of effort or sincere desire for a better relationship and not because her husband didn't *want* to feel closer to her.

That's right. Mark wanted to feel closer to her as much as she wanted to feel closer to him, even though he resisted, undermined, and outright sabotaged her noble, if misguided efforts to bring them closer. When we use this example in workshops, female participants are quick to condemn Mark (and vicariously their own partners). "He should be ashamed of himself," they say with no small degree of passion. But, remember, shame is the *problem,* not the solution. He *was* ashamed of himself, and that's why he resisted, undermined, and sabotaged Marlene's efforts.

Marlene made two mistakes. Her first was to use a formula for change that came from women's magazines, self-help books, counselors, and weekend retreats designed to appeal to women. Her second mistake was to misunderstand how human beings undergo emotional change and how they maintain it in the routine of daily living.

Marlene looked for lasting change to come in a huge wave of emotion. You may have noticed in your own experience that men are pretty reluctant to give in to big waves of emotion. But even when they do, the effects will not last. Relationship changes that occur in large waves are doomed to failure when the waves subside. Things like hot seduction, romantic weekends, emotionally charged marriage retreats, and cathartic therapy sessions may have some temporary effects but will never help *sustain* a close connection with a man. **Permanent change has to become part of his daily routine.** Men like routine, because it helps them ease into their emotions. Women, if you want to feel more love from the man in your life, honor his routine.

Why Men Need Routine

Routine is an area that requires women to take a leap of faith to understand. The majority of one thousand women polled on the street would not express a longing for more routine in their relationships. But men would. Men love routine for this important reason: It reduces the risk of abrupt arousal and the shame that comes immediately after it. The way routine reduces shame is *indirect,* due more to a neurological difference in the way men and women process information than to individual personalities or relationship dynamics.

Research shows that women do a lot more multitasking and are much better at it than men. Multitasking is the ability to do one thing competently while thinking about doing another thing and, at the same time, planning what you'll do next. In general (attention deficit disorders aside), women multitask better, and men focus better. A woman can get up in the morning, decide what she wants for breakfast, get the kids ready for school, and think about how she's going to advise her girlfriend who's in a bad relationship, all while listening for the timer on the dryer to go off so the clothes don't get wrinkled. A man gets up in the morning and has the same thing for breakfast he has every day so he won't have to use energy thinking about what to eat, sits down and reads the paper and doesn't interact with anyone because he can't do both, leaves the house at the same time so he doesn't have to worry about whether he's going to be late, and takes the same route to work, and so on, all so he can save his energy to focus on one thing at a time. When you ask a man to watch the children, he often asks, "What should I do with them?" To him, *watch* the children means you can't do anything else. Women, on the other hand, complete multiple tasks *while* watching the children. That's why men play with children more than women—if he's going to watch, he might as well *do something* with them.

Now here's how all this all relates to routine and the reduction of shame in men. When tasks are done repeatedly, they can be completed on *automatic pilot,* without much attention. For instance, it takes a long time to learn how to drive, but once you learn, you can do it without thinking about it. In fact, once driving becomes routine, you think about everything except driving. The more things a man can do by routine, the less he will have to focus on the routine things he's doing, which is an adaptive way for him to use his ability to focus to optimal advantage. When a man breaks his routine, he loses focus, which makes him feel that he will not accomplish tasks as competently. In other words, he begins to feel like a failure and has to suffer the cortisol curse that goes with failing. Here's an example.

Maya often misplaces her keys when changing her purse to match her outfit. She then borrows her husband James's keys, because they are *routinely* located in a dish on the kitchen counter. This drives James crazy. Maya thinks, "What's the big deal? Why are you getting all whacked out over keys?" Maya doesn't realize that when James reaches for his keys on his way out the door and finds them missing, this abrupt annoyance sends an chemical shock throughout his system. This means he has to deal with the cortisol curse and resulting hyperarousal hangover for the next several hours.

Honoring a man's routine, as well as his quiet, uninterrupted time at home, with understanding and support of his need for his own time, is a powerful way of showing love to him. It's as powerful for him as a deep intimate conversation is for her. This point came as an aha moment to Jeannine, who couldn't understand why her husband got sulky, if not upset, when she wanted to leave the house. "Why do you mind if I go?" she asked, sometimes accusingly. "You weren't doing anything with me anyway." What she didn't grasp is that her presence alone made him feel connected while he was cruising along in his own rhythm. Most women do not get this crucial point: Men feel happier and more secure at home when their wives are there with them. And the reason they feel this way is that their wives provide the meaning of life. The man's routine *works* when she's there.

The longing of men for the stability of their wives' presence is, unfortunately, often mistaken for control. Indeed, it can easily cross the line into controlling behavior, if you and your partner are not careful. Having worked with couples on many variations of this problem, we offer the following example, a composite of several different cases.

Now that the kids are in school, Maria wants to take graduate courses in preparation for a new career. She and Toby had agreed to this plan before their twins were born, and he had always been supportive of her dreams. But as the registration deadline grew closer, he began to withdraw and sulk. In her excitement about her new life, Maria didn't notice at first. When she finally did notice, Toby denied there was anything wrong, so she let it go. But just before she was going to register, Toby erupted in a rage over the electric bill, which was just a little bit higher than usual. Thinking that his distress might have been caused by the extra expenses involved in graduate school, she reminded him that they had already saved the money to pay for it, which introduced provider-shame into the equation. Though usually a safe bet when a man mentions bills, this time it wasn't about money at all. Toby immediately accused her of abandoning their children and the responsibilities of their marriage by taking classes at night.

Was this a classic case of a man trying to restrict the advancement of his wife, in what might be described as the patriarchal drive of men to oppress women? We didn't think so. We believed Toby when he said he was proud of Maria and wanted what was best for her. But when the time for the change drew near, he felt that he was losing something more important than his ability to control her—he felt he was losing the *stability* she provided for him while they were home together. Her plan was to take classes at night while he watched the kids, which meant that they would have no time together all week. He didn't mind taking care of the kids while she did course work on the weekends. He minded not having time with Maria. So in this case, the easy solution was for Maria to take classes during the day. It turned out that her university, like many these days, was sensitive to mothers pursuing degrees and provided low-cost after-school care for the kids. Thus she was home most nights, doing her homework in one room, while Toby did his routine with the kids in another. This enabled them to feel more connected, while they supported each other's doing "their own thing."

Here's our advice to women: Honor a man's need for routine and understand that, when you support his routine, he feels loved by you and connected to you. For example, leave the car keys on the hook where they belong every day or, if you do the shopping, make sure his favorite brand of coffee and cereal are available each morning.

Here's our advice to men: Incorporate gestures of connection into your daily routine. For example, before pouring the milk on the same cereal you eat every morning, hug her; before leaving the house for work at the same time each morning, kiss her good-bye. Realize how much she means to you *now,* before she walks out the door.

Why Does a Man Fall in Love with His Wife as She Walks out the Door?

No, it's not the irresistibility of her rear end framed by suitcases, it's just that, as a rule, you think about a secure base only when it becomes *insecure.* For instance, your home is a secure base, but you take it for granted unless there's a threat of losing it or it needs repair or when there's a storm coming. When it just sits on its lot waiting patiently for you to come home, you hardly ever think about it. It's pretty much the same with your relationship. When you are getting along, feeling close and connected, you don't think about each other much when you are at work or busy with other tasks. Oh, you might have a brief, *pleasant* thought, but you go right back to sharp focus on your work or whatever you were doing. But when things are going poorly, you can't get it out of your mind! Not only are you thinking of all the stupid things he or she did yesterday to make your life miserable but also you have a whole rap sheet of misdemeanors from the last twelve years to keep your thoughts occupied for hours. This obsessive quality of resentment is why we work less efficiently, with higher error rates, when our relationships are not strong and we're not connected to our partners. It's also why research shows that people work at their best, with maximum concentration and efficiency, when their relationships are the strongest—but it's *so* easy to take this for granted!

Sometimes it seems as if our partners purposely cause resentment just to get us to think about them more, but that is definitely not the case. We don't need them to undermine us, because we do such a great job of it ourselves, *by thinking about security only in times of insecurity.* If we blame the early signs of insecurity in the relationship on our partners, then we get resentful, and of course they do the same. Women stop asking for attention and start demanding it (nagging), then stop demanding and start attacking, then stop attacking and start thinking about leaving. (A quiet woman is a bad sign!) Having failed to respond to her requests when the relationship was secure, he reacts to her demands as if they were attacks on his secure base either by stonewalling or by launching attacks of his own.

By the time men accept that their secure base has become insecure and that they have to do something to strengthen it, it's often too late. We've seen hundreds of men fall in love with their wives as they walk out the door.

When men leave a relationship first, they almost always have another woman lined up or at least have their eye on one, which is why the dreadful loss of meaning and isolation doesn't occur to them—they have somebody else to fill the void. This is hardly ever the case with women. By the time they are ready to leave, another man is the last thing they want for a while. When men leave the marriage, they often do it on impulse and end up renting a room or staying with a friend. They usually think of the separation as temporary. "Well, if my life doesn't work out, I can always go back home." In contrast, a woman leaves at the end of a long, deliberative process in which she has agonized over all the things she will lose and all the bad things that might happen because of divorce. So by the time she is ready to walk out the door, she is resolved and unlikely to return.

Why Doesn't He Get It Before It's Too Late?

Women ask: Why doesn't he think about how his life would be without me? He's seen what happens to men he knows when their relationships end. Why doesn't he think about sleeping alone, eating alone, and sitting at home alone, utterly cut off from everything he loves? She can't understand why he doesn't get it before it's too late. She ends up tragically concluding that he just doesn't care. What is even more confusing is *she doesn't understand that* he *doesn't understand*. Once again, the true culprit is the difference in how we cope with fear and shame.

Women tend to regulate anxiety by considering the future and figuring out what they will do if bad things happen. They will not only think about the details of divorced living but also obsess about them, which is why it takes them so long to make up their minds to leave. But when your primary vulnerability is shame, you try to *avoid* thinking about anything that invokes a sense of failure and inadequacy. It's not that men ignore what will happen when they're divorced, it's that their defenses do not allow those failure-provoking thoughts to enter consciousness. **Fear puts thoughts into your consciousness; shame keeps thoughts out of it.** What looks to women like an uncaring, immovable object of a man is often just a guy doing his best to avoid the overwhelming hopelessness of feeling ashamed. We realize that we're asking women to take another leap of faith. We're asking you to see the behaviors you now think of as uncaring, uninvolved, or shut down as coming from a man who holds you at the center of his universe and cannot fathom life without you. Thoughts of life without you are so horrible that he can't bear to think them. If he can't bear to think them, he can't begin to talk to you about them. This is the primary reason you can't have talks with him about emotionally charged issues like you can with your girlfriends. Here are some others.

The Emotional Vocabulary Gap:
Why It Sounds Phony When *He* Does It

Having a working emotional vocabulary is more than just knowing the meaning of words. It includes the ability to label, describe, and express your varied and subtle emotions and to interpret the emotional expressions of other people. Females seem to have a brain structure that is a bit more suited to emotional vocabulary. They have more cells in the areas of the brain that mediate language and that connect the emotional areas with the language areas. This slight biological difference is apparent in the verbal behavior of children as young as eighteen months.* It becomes greatly exaggerated by parenting, peers, school, and culture as we talk about emotions and use emotional words far more with little girls than little boys.

By the end of the language-imprinting period—the first seven years of life—most girls are able to use words to forge emotional connections. A seven-year-old girl is likely to have a more active emotional vocabulary than her father. It has nothing to do with intelligence or maturity. Men know the meaning of the words; they just don't use them to make emotional connection the way females do. Emotional talk is the native language of females, leading one anthropologist to observe that talking is to women what grooming is to other primates.

Teaching adult men emotional vocabulary will *never* give them the verbal fluency of women, just as learning a new language in adulthood cannot match learning it as a child and speaking it throughout life. Emotional words are a second language for him, and he'll speak it with a thick accent. No matter how much he tries, he just won't sound as natural and genuine as your girlfriends using the same words.†

*Interestingly, the decided female advantage in verbal skills at eighteen months disappears when the mother is given a testosterone shot in the last trimester of her pregnancy.

†Even men who are highly skilled at writing, like poets and novelists, are not good applying their language skill in their marriages. They tend to be narcissistic in their use of emotional vocabulary and unable to relate it to people close to them. In other words, they can use language to connect to themselves and to people in the abstract but not to those close to them.

Relying on verbal exchange to gain intimacy with a man can make connection seem less genuine and satisfying.

Women readers are probably thinking that he doesn't have to get the words right as long as he speaks from his heart. Surely when a man speaks from his heart, he will expose whatever vulnerability is there in the same way a woman does, and that will help both of you forge a deeper level of intimacy. That sounds so good on paper that Steven, who has counseled thousands of men, used to urge his clients to do just that. "Tell her that sometimes you feel like your job and other burdens seem to be too much for you and that you feel like a failure sometimes—give her a chance to be supportive." Well, Steven should have known better and realized that when a man expresses his dread of failure, his partner is likely to react with her *own* vulnerability. He finally got it by around the tenth time he heard this response from a man who followed his advice:

"I told her how I feel about my job, and her first reaction was 'Oh no, we're going to lose our house!' " Most men stop at the first sign of rising anxiety in the woman, but a few persist, only to hear things like "Why can't you be like Joe; he has a great a job and doesn't make his wife worry." This kind of remark is an anxiety reaction on the part of these women, not an intentional attack, but it is nevertheless devastating to a man.

The disconnect of what women *think* they want to hear from their partners and what they can tolerate without increased anxiety doesn't just apply to core vulnerabilities, as we'll see in the next section.

Not *Those* Feelings!

You want your man to express his feelings? Be careful what you wish for!

"I just want to know what he's feeling" is the common female request at the beginning of marriage therapy. "He's so closed off."

"I'm not feeling anything, I'm just tired" is the usual reply.

Like most counselors, we used to work hard, sometimes spending many hours with men alone to "get them in touch with their feelings." Eventually we'd succeed, only to find that once he'd gotten more expressive about his feelings, his partner was even more dissatisfied. What she didn't understand is that exploring feelings makes them more complex, and complexity has a way of turning into demands.

"I thought I was just tired," says the guy newly in touch with his feelings, "but I'm really sad, lonely, ambivalent, distant, mournful, neglected, burdened, unappreciated, mistreated, taken advantage of, etc. I have a lot of *needs* that are not getting *met* in this relationship!"

Of course his partner would respond with exasperation.

"But you wanted him to express his feelings," we would say.

"Not *those* feelings!" she'd exclaim in disgust. "I want to hear how much he loves me and how important I am to him and how empty and sad his life would be without me."

Here is a tough question that women need to ask themselves: Do you really want to know about his feelings or do you merely want him to validate yours and comply with your idea of connection?

As we write this, Pat recalls a client, Heather, who got exactly what she'd asked for and this is what happened.

"I never know what's going on inside him," Heather complained. "He never shows his feelings. I don't know what he's thinking. I just don't understand how he could love me and be so unresponsive and inconsiderate." Jeff sat silently as Heather talked.

Pat cut Heather off, turned to Jeff, and asked, "How can I be of help to *you*?"

Jeff replied, "I want our relationship to be like it was in the beginning. The beginning of our relationship was the happiest time in my life. It was fun, I felt like she really loved me. . . ." He paused, then said with a slight blush, "And the sex was great."

Heather interrupted, "You were different in the beginning. You talked to me—"

Pat interrupted Heather and asked, "Do you miss the good times, Jeff?"

"Yes," he said with sadness.

"What do you miss the most?" Pat pursued.

"I miss being lovers. I miss having it be easy. . . ." Then he paused, looking down at the floor. "I miss everything about that time." Jeff's eyes began to glisten, red splotches appeared on his cheeks and neck, and his chin began to quiver. He took a risk by expressing his emotions. Pat felt hopeful, knowing this was exactly what Heather had asked for, but when she turned to her, hoping to see her drinking in the moment, Heather was reading the book titles on the shelf! She had checked out, abruptly shifted her interest, and missed the very thing she had asked for. Why? Because her preconceived notion of connection was female—she wanted him to listen to *her* and validate her feelings and view connection the way that she does—the way that she has it with her girlfriends. Jeff was talking about the male form of connection—doing things together and making love.

Again we remind women, be careful what you ask for, because if you refuse the connection when he extends the olive branch, you will make it difficult—if not impossible—for him to give you what you're asking for. It's a common request of women to ask men to share their thoughts and feelings. The need driving this request is the need for connection. Women know they're connected to their girlfriends when they share feelings, but when men share their feelings they expose their vulnerability. If you expect a man to be forthcoming with his feelings, you must cease all the distraction, impatience, criticism, and other forms of stomping on his heart that taught him in the past that it is not safe to go there.

Do You Want Him to Be Another Girlfriend or Do You Want to Be Closer to *Him*?

Women typically connect with each other by one of them *exposing* vulnerability. They communicate, in words or body language, that they feel anxious, worried, upset, sad, disregarded, or taken for granted. The girlfriend shows understanding by revealing her own vulnerability—and they feel connected. But men, as we have seen, are conditioned early in life to *hide* vulnerability. So when a woman tells him that she feels bad, he gets impatient at best or, worse, feels accused and inadequate. That makes him want to ignore her, tell her what to do, or just leave the room before he gets himself into more trouble. It can get worse if she starts to analyze his response. Unlike her girlfriends, men *hate* to be analyzed. And what they hate most of all is to be *psychoanalyzed,* as in: "You're uncomfortable with my feelings because your dad never made your mom happy." And if he doesn't agree with her analysis, he's "in denial."

Is the Content of His Talk Really That Different Now?

Many women are under the illusion that their husbands talked about their feelings all the time when they were courting and suddenly developed a disorder of emotional vocabulary soon after the wedding. Research shows that there's no difference in the word choice or sentence structure of men before and after marriage, *until* a pall of resentment starts to settle on the household, in which case both parties are reduced to chronic criticism, defensiveness, and stonewalling. It was not the content of your talks before marriage that was so different, it was the high level of mutual interest you had in each other. You were emotionally connected then, and you're not now. Lack of connection is the true source of the resentment in your relationship. Your disconnection has been caused by misunderstanding fear and shame. That is so unfortunate, because nothing soothes fear and shame like connection.

Connection Reduces Fear and Shame

Women, your guys' word choices weren't any different when you first fell in love, but he found it easier to be open emotionally then because your connection reduced his vulnerability to shame. What's more, your current disconnection has raised your anxiety, which makes you want to talk about emotions more now than you did then. In courtship you didn't require as much talk about feelings because you had what you wanted. Remember, the goal of talking about feelings is to feel connected. If you *are* connected, it becomes unnecessary to talk about feelings. When it's unnecessary to do so, men sometimes find it fun to talk about emotions. No doubt many of your more emotional talks have occurred after sex, when he felt connected to you.

We communicate well with our intimate partners when we feel connected and poorly when we don't. When you feel connected again, your desire to explore feelings with your partner will practically vanish. It's a great combination: He'll be able to do more of it, you'll want less of it, and you'll meet in the middle.

The bottom line is, think *connection,* not *communication.* Then you won't shame him and he won't make you afraid. Nor will he drive you away. Instead, he'll fall back in love with you long before you walk out the door.

The silent male needs to feel connected to his life partner, as much as she needs to feel connected to him. But the expression of that need is different for each of them. He feels ashamed to tell her that her mere presence, even in the next room, is soothing, stabilizing, and important to him. He is ashamed to tell her that he can get easily overwhelmed by his emotions if she is too direct too quickly. In addition, he doesn't quite have the words to tell her that she makes his work, along with almost everything else in his life, more meaningful. He needs to understand that she does not try to hassle or nag him or point out his "failings" or impinge upon his privacy. Rather, she is trying to reconnect with him because he is important to her. They are important to each other, although their shame and fear make them lose sight of how important.

In the next three chapters, we'll consider what happens when neither you nor your partner realizes your enormous power to protect each other from your vulnerability to fear and shame.

the worst thing a woman does to a man

Shaming

On average, men have more physical strength than women. The male thumb, for example, can be up to thirty times stronger than the female thumb (better for channel surfing!). Because of this physical difference, society has developed mores to accommodate and sometimes exploit the male strength. Men take on more dangerous jobs (and therefore are injured and killed more often). They're expected to carry heavy parcels, open doors, and walk on the sidewalk closer to the curb to intercept incoming mud or straying vehicles. When two buddies greet each other, they often flaunt this physical prowess with a punch in the arm or a slap on the back. On the other hand, a man *withholds* his strength when greeting a woman. He offers a gentle handshake or an affectionate hug.

Masculine physiology powerfully enhances the negative effects of resentful or angry behavior. The males of all species of social animals have greater muscle mass; quicker reflexes; and deeper, more resonant voices, specifically designed for *roaring*. The angry male voice gets deeper, louder, and more menacing, because it is designed to invoke fear of physical harm, whether he wants it to or not. Angry women can sound shrill or unpleasant, but rarely will their voices invoke fear of physical harm in grown men. Angry or resentful males—of all species of social mammals—experience considerably more blood flow to their muscles and higher levels of central nervous system activity than angry females, making their bodies more of a physical threat. Because of their physical prowess, male social animals, including early humans, developed a defensive strategy of forming perimeters around the threatened tribe or pack; and puffing up their muscles and roaring to warn, threaten, intimidate, and invoke fear in potential opponents. This instinctual strategy has obvious survival advantages for women under male care. It has obvious disadvantages for a woman, however, if the male uses his physical strength *against* her. For this reason, during the past three decades, we have developed laws and rules to constrain male physical strength, specifically in regard to women. Everyone agrees that it is wrong for men to exploit the vulnerability of women by doing anything that might invoke fear. But there are no such laws to constrain the female advantage in verbal strength, specifically in regard to exploiting male vulnerability to shame.

Words hurt. Words destroy. Words can kill a relationship.

When Pat did the research for her book with Jo Robinson, *Hot Monogamy,* she interviewed fifteen hundred couples regarding relationships. Several surprising pieces of information came out of that research, and three of them are very relevant to this book.

1. Most women do not understand how much it pleases a man to please a woman, specifically how important it is to the man in her life to please her. Furthermore, a man does not simply want to please her—he *lives* to please her.

2. Women can easily see how frightening men are to them because of the threat of physical abuse, but they do not see their own power to evoke shame.

3. What women often interpret as withdrawn, uncaring men, for the most part, are men overwhelmed by the criticism and unhappiness coming from their partners.

Many women have no clue how critical and demeaning they are to men. When confronted with their critical behavior, the most common reaction is disbelief. "I'm just trying to make him a better person!"—that is, more thoughtful, considerate, responsible, reliable, and so on. Reflecting on this fact, Pat thought it might be interesting to list 101 ways to shame a man without trying. Off the top of her head, she came up with well over fifty ways she had done so, inadvertently or otherwise, in her own relationships. Here are a few:

- Excluding him from important decisions: "I told my sister we would vacation with them this year."
- Robbing him of the opportunity to help (by overfunctioning and overdoing): "Don't bother—I'll do it."
- Correcting what he said: "It was last Wednesday, not Thursday."
- Questioning his judgment: "Are you going to cook those eggs one at a time?"
- Giving unsolicited advice: "If you would just make the call you'll feel better."
- Ignoring his advice: "This is woman's stuff—you really don't know anything about it."
- Implying inadequacy: "I wish you had been at that workshop with me" (not because he would have enjoyed it but because it would have "corrected some of his flaws").
- Making unrealistic demands of his time and energy: "After you rotate the tires and paint the shed, I want you to listen to how my day was."
- Overreacting (which is a form of criticizing his choices or behavior): "I can't believe you voted for him!"
- Ignoring his needs (basically sending the message that they're not important): "You're not that tired; anyway, having company will give you energy."
- Focusing on what I didn't get, not what I did: "It would have been better if you'd said 'I'm sorry' to begin with."
- Withholding praise: "Well, it's your *job* to mow the lawn."
- Using a harsh tone: "I am so tired of this!"

* Valuing others' needs over his: Saying to a friend, "Oh, he's not too tired to come pick you up and then take you back home after we have a nice visit."
* Undermining his wishes: Saying to a relative, "I agreed to have a quiet Thanksgiving, but if you invite us, he couldn't say no."
* Condescending: "You did an okay job picking out your shirt."
* Name-calling: "You're such a negative person."
* Belittling his work: "Just what is it you *do* all day?"
* Showing little or no interest in his interests: "I can't imagine what you see in that."
* Criticizing his family: "Your sister didn't even offer to help clean up the kitchen!"
* Ignoring him: Choosing friends over his company.
* Interpreting him: "What you really meant when you said you were tired is that you don't want to listen to me."
* Comparing: "The neighbor's yard sure looks nice."
* Dismissing: "I have to work" (implying he doesn't).
* Focusing on my own unhappiness: "I can't live this way."
* Expecting him to make me happy: "If we just did more fun things together . . ."
* Making "you" statements: "You make me so mad I can't think straight!"
* Globalizing: "Men are not capable of understanding!"
* Generalizing: "You're always criticizing me."
* Therapizing: "You are trying to make up for your father."
* Projecting my unhappiness on him: "I feel bad when *I* don't talk, so you can't possibly feel okay if you're this quiet."

Other shaming favorites of women include:

* Believing they always know what's best for the relationship
* Rolling eyes
* Giving "the look"

- Being sarcastic
- Ridiculing
- Suggesting a "better way"
- Having unrealistic expectations
- Criticizing him in front of other people
- Making him feel unnecessary

If you are a woman reading this and thinking "I don't shame," you may be right. But just to make sure, check it out with the men in your life. It's best not to ask directly. Don't say, "Do I criticize?" or "Do I shame you?" That's like asking "Does my butt look big in this dress?" No guy in his right mind is going to give you a straight answer. Instead, ask: "What are some of the different ways I criticize or shame you?"

For an eye-opener, write "true" or "false" next to each of the following statements (choose "true" if it applies to you at least sometimes):

1. I exclude him from important decisions. _____
2. I don't always give him a chance to help. _____
3. I correct things he says. _____
4. I question his judgment. _____
5. I give him unsolicited advice. _____
6. I suggest how he *should* feel. _____
7. I ignore his advice. _____
8. I imply that he's inadequate in certain areas. _____
9. I'm often in a bad mood. _____
10. I think that he should at least match my use of time and energy. _____
11. When he says I overreact, I think that he just doesn't get it. _____
12. I ignore his needs that I think aren't important. _____
13. I focus on what I don't have instead of what I have. _____

14. I withhold praise because I think he doesn't really deserve
    it or because I don't want him to get a big head. _____

15. I use a harsh tone to get through to him. _____

16. I pay more attention to other people's needs than to his. _____

17. I undermine his wishes. _____

18. I am condescending to him. _____

19. I lack respect for his work. _____

20. I show little interest in his interests. _____

21. I criticize his family. _____

22. I interpret the "real meaning" of what he says and does. _____

23. I compare him to other men or, worse, to my girlfriends. _____

24. I don't take his point of view seriously. _____

25. I believe he just can't see my unhappiness. _____

26. I think he fails to make me happy. _____

26. If I'm unhappy, I tell him that he must be unhappy, too. _____

28. I roll my eyes when I think of some of the things he
    says and does. _____

29. He says I give him "the look." _____

30. I am sometimes sarcastic to make my point or express
    my dissatisfaction with his behavior. _____

31. I use ridicule to get through to him. _____

32. I usually have a "better way" of doing things. _____

33. Sometimes I think he's a jerk. _____

34. I have to tell him what he's doing wrong. _____

35. I tell him that he never helps me enough. _____

36. He can't handle my feelings. _____

37. I believe that if his childhood or previous relationships
    were different, we wouldn't have these problems. _____

38. I think that I understand relationships better than he does. _____

39. I think I do more than he does. _____

40. My friends treat me better than he does. _____

41. He disappoints me. _____

Total of "true" answers _____

Now ask him to fill out the same quiz to see if *he* thinks you do any of those things.

When a woman criticizes a man, whether she does it deliberately or not, she makes it impossible for him to feel connected to her. Where there is a withdrawn or silent man, there is usually a critical woman.

Hopefully you've gotten the idea by now that women can do great harm to their relationships without even realizing it. The next chapter highlights how men can do the same. Please understand that the purpose of these two chapters is not to divvy up blame but to point out that we all fall prey to the fear-shame dynamic when it's allowed to run on automatic pilot. The extent to which we can understand and sympathize with each other's hidden vulnerability to fear and shame will determine our success in finding love beyond words.

the worst thing a
man does to a woman

Leaving Her Alone but Married

While public records show the majority of divorces are filed by women, most women will tell you that *he* left the relationship long before *she* did. What makes marriage miserable for a woman is the isolation she feels when her husband seems to leave the marriage emotionally—a defense against shame. One woman said it best: "I have the worst of both worlds. I have the loneliness of being single and the constraints of being married. I can't go out and date, but I don't have the support and attention of a partner." Women who leave commonly report some version of this *alone-but-married syndrome*. Here are some examples of how men drive women away, most of the time without ever meaning to.

Alone at Home

Even though men have picked up some of the slack in household chores over the past ten years, women still do the lion's share at home. Although most of the time she has a job just like he does, she still has a larger portion of the responsibility for doing housework; preparing meals; entertaining; maintaining family ties; decorating the home; shopping; organizing seasonal celebrations, birthdays, and cultural and social events; and making dental and medical appointments. And that's if you don't add kids or pets to the list, which bring new responsibilities, most of which fall under her job description. But it's not just the workload that gets a woman down. It is the feeling that she is the *only one responsible for all there is to be done.* Many men still don't understand how much time and effort it takes to keep a home running smoothly: for example, putting in a new roll of toilet paper when the one on the spool runs out or putting your dirty clothes in the laundry basket instead of tossing them on the chair or floor. All too often when a man does housework it's a *favor.* When a woman does housework it's *forgotten.*

Sometimes men fail to appreciate and share household burdens out of sheer obliviousness. But if they are irritable about it or feel entitled, resentful, or angry, shame is almost always at the core. They either feel guilty—in their hearts they know they *should* do more—or unappreciated for *their* contributions. Once again, the primary way men deal with shame is to *avoid* whatever invokes it, while the primary way women deal with fear is to *talk* about it.

Alone in Her Dreams

When two people fall in love, they begin to dream of a life together. Sometimes this dream is conscious, sometimes unconscious.

When Amelia met Marcus, part of the dream she began to weave was to have financial stability. Growing up in rural New Mexico in a family that constantly struggled to make ends meet made a lasting impression on her. She looked forward to building financial security with Marcus and was more than willing to do her share to make that happen. When they married, she chose a simple, inexpensive ceremony so they could use the money they saved toward a down payment on a house. After six years of frugal living, they had enough money to buy out her brother-in-law's share of their small family-owned dry cleaning business. Amelia and Marcus ran the business together for three years, but once she got pregnant, Amelia took time off to be a stay-at-home mom, and because the second baby came along sooner than planned, five years passed with Marcus running the business alone.

One day Marcus came home visibly upset. There was yet another delay in the delivery of cleaning chemicals that were vital to running the family business. "Today was the last straw. For the third time, NuChem didn't show up. I called Jim Callahan and told him I was buying into a distributorship with him starting in two weeks."

Amelia would report years later that when Marcus made this pronouncement, it felt like the beginning of the end for her. "I knew my need for financial security didn't matter to him. He risked everything we had without even talking to me."

Marcus thought his unilateral decision was only about business. In reality, it had the effect of leaving Amelia alone in her dream for financial security and exposing her to her fear of deprivation and isolation.

This true story illustrates an important fact: Men don't realize that a woman's fear of isolation and deprivation can be triggered by leaving her out of any number of important aspects of his life. Here are some real-life examples of ignored dreams that drove women away from the men in their lives. He left her:

- Alone in her dream to own a home
- Alone in her dream to have a faithful husband
- Alone in her dream for a large, loving family
- Alone in her dream to be active as a couple
- Alone in her dream to be seen as an equal
- Alone in her dream to have a place in his life where his mother could not interfere
- Alone in her dream for a home without angry outbursts
- Alone in her dream to have a romantic partner
- Alone in her dream to be respected in her work

Just as Marcus left Amelia out of his business decision, men who do any of the above are abandoning their wives in order to manage their own dread of failing as a provider, protector, lover, or parent. A man needs to value the longing of a woman's heart, or he will leave her alone in her dreams and become the failure he dreads.

Alone on the Outside of His Life

Men and women in the United States work longer hours than in any other industrialized nation, including Japan, which gave us the term *karoshi,* meaning "to drop dead from overwork." We actually work longer hours than the serfs did in the Dark Ages. And now with telecommunication, work doesn't stop when you leave the workplace. Evening and weekend hours that used to belong to the individual and family are increasingly considered fair game for getting caught up at work. But of course with most jobs you can never get caught up. Precious few workdays end with getting everything done. Instead, you just have to quit and face the load the next day. The result of this never-ending workday is less and less time for recuperating and relaxing, giving the phrase "I gave at the office" a whole new meaning. It's not just time you donate at work, it's the overwhelming majority of your life energy.

Unprecedented work expectations affect women as well as men; *everyone* is tired at the end of a workday. The question is: How does a man choose to recuperate from the stress of work? Does he go straight from work to happy hour with coworkers or buddies? Does he come home and withdraw into his own world? Does he use silence, TV, the computer, or individual hobbies that exclude her? Does he come home with an attitude that says *I've worked all day and now I deserve to rest and be by myself*? Does he use the weekend to pursue activities that are of no interest to her? If so, he is leaving her on the outside of his world.

Many men *feel* like they carry an extra burden of work. Despite the fact that their wives work more, it seems that work is harder on them as men. This is due not to any sense of fairness but to their dread of failing as providers. Ashamed to admit it to their wives, they cover it up with a sense of entitlement: "I have the *right* to relax in my own home." This keeps their wives on the outside of their world and jeopardizes the most important thing in their lives—their relationship.

Alone in Bed

Many men don't realize how they take the fun out of sex. In the beginning of a relationship women like sex, they want sex, and they are full of sexual energy. So what happens? Here are six common ways women say men leave them alone in bed.

1. They confuse sex with intimacy. *My husband has the one-stop-shopping approach to sex. He figures he can give me attention, get credit for being intimate, meet my needs for touching, be romantic, spend quality time with me, and make me a happy camper—all by having sex. Once that is over, I'm on my own.*

2. It's all about him. *Sex means one thing—his orgasm. He doesn't ask if I've had an orgasm or if I'm satisfied. There is so little foreplay that I feel like I have to do it all myself. Even though I enjoy sex and want sex, I've become so resentful about his attitude that it has become more and more difficult to even enjoy sex.*

3. Sex is the only time he shows interest. *I always know when my husband wants sex, because that's the only time he's affectionate. If he puts his arm around me or touches me, that's his way of saying it's time for sex. He has no idea how obvious he is. I feel like he's only interested in me when he wants to have sex. Otherwise he's in his own world.*

4. He devalues sex by making it crude. *If sex is going to be a special experience for the two of us, I can't reconcile that with making crude sexual jokes and constant sexual innuendos. To me, sex is a sacred act between a man and*

a woman; it's such a turnoff to make it into a dirty joke. And, for sure, farting isn't foreplay.

5. He expects me to be like him. *My husband doesn't understand that for me sex has to have an emotional connection that is built on kindness and respect. Without that base I can't get sexually aroused. Even when I do feel close to him, it takes me a while to get excited sexually. I can't get there in five minutes, the way he can. I've never been able to make him understand that it takes more time and attention for me.*

6. He neglects me sexually. *I'm in the awkward position of being the only woman among my friends who wants sex more than her husband. My girlfriends complain all the time about their husband's insatiable sexual appetite while I am left high and dry. We have a role reversal. I want sex, but he doesn't. What does he expect me to do with my sexual needs? I truly am alone in bed.*

The male problem with sexuality is due almost entirely to his hypersensitivity to shame. Our culture heaps a lot of shame on sex, period. And this has profound effects on both men and women. However, lack of intimacy and emotional sharing in sex tends to be more of a male issue. Women like to think of themselves as being sexually desirable or sexual *attractors*. Men like to think of themselves as studs or sexual *performers*. Of course, women like giving pleasure to men, but they are not likely to think of themselves as less of a woman if it doesn't go perfectly. "Womanhood" is rarely at stake in sexual encounters, whereas "manhood," in the mind of the man at least, is very often at risk. (Any woman who has read at least one romance novel is familiar with the term "throbbing manhood," which doesn't refer to the size of his intellect.) All of the above-described ways that men leave women alone in bed are attempts to reduce his dread of sexual inadequacy. If he pretends you don't have needs, he doesn't have to face the pain of failing you. Until a man changes the way he avoids sexual embarrassment or shame, he runs the risk of leaving a woman alone in bed.

Alone on the Edge of His Depression

Depression affects over fifty million people in the United States, but despite this high incidence, few people have an accurate understanding of this very treatable disease. Nor do many people understand the havoc depression can wreak on a relationship. Men as well as women suffer from depression, but far more women seek help. This leaves many women alone on the edge of his depression. A survey showing public perceptions of the cause of depression explains why it is difficult for men to seek help—most people see it as a shameful thing:

- 71 percent believe depression is due to emotional weakness.
- 65 percent believe depression is caused by bad parenting.
- 45 percent believe depression is a personal choice.
- 43 percent believe depression is incurable.
- 35 percent believe depression is the consequence of sin.

The truth about depression is that it has many causes, including genetic predisposition, lifestyle, stress, and individual coping styles. Fortunately, it is highly treatable, which is good news given how destructive it can be to relationships. When one person in a relationship is depressed, the divorce rate goes up *nine* times! The reasons for this startling fact lie in the symptoms of depression. Imagine living with someone who:

- Has little interest in self or others
- Withdraws
- Has a negative attitude
- Blames others
- Procrastinates
- Overreacts to simple issues
- Cries easily and often
- Has unpredictable mood swings

- Lacks sexual interest
- Is hyperfocused on sex
- Doesn't feel the effects of love
- Gets jealous easily and often
- Is paranoid
- Uses passive-aggressive behavior
- Is prone to irritability, anger, aggression, and/or rage
- Takes inordinate risks
- Is insensitive to others
- Does not seem to care
- Is continually dissatisfied
- Is chronically unhappy

Many people erroneously believe depression comes from bad relationships, while it is far more accurate to say that *bad relationships come from untreated depression*. Again, depression is highly treatable, not only with medication but also with diet, supplements, hormones, exercise, outdoor activity, healthy coping strategies, and lifestyle changes. Many men regard help seeking of any kind as a sure sign of inadequacy, but to seek help for mental health problems is particularly shameful, because *their role is to be strong*—physically and *mentally*. This is why he's likely to get angry at his wife for even implying that he might be depressed. What he hears is *You are a failure.* If she dares suggest that he see someone for his depression, he will likely perceive it as an attack and launch his own counterattack. We cannot emphasize this issue enough. Research clearly shows that, unless depression is addressed and alleviated, the woman will not only be left alone on the edge of his depression; sooner or later she will be gone.

Alone in Her Fears

Perhaps the most stressful form of isolation for a woman occurs when the person she would normally turn to for comfort is the source of threat. Men are frightening to women because of their brute strength and the heart-stopping force of their anger. Most men have no idea how frightening, threatening, and terrorizing their anger is to women. Even when the anger is not directed at the woman, it still has a frightening effect. An angry voice can trigger her fear response and dump cortisol into her system. If he has a habit of overreacting and getting angry on a regular basis, she lives in a constant state of fear and alertness. In addition, she cannot feel completely safe or relaxed with him—a prerequisite for love, affection, and *connection*.

A man can never completely understand a woman's fear response, just as she can never completely understand his vulnerability to shame. He must take her at her word and regulate his anger, which most often rises from some unconscious and irrational sense that he's failing. Otherwise, he will leave her alone in her fear and eventually destroy the relationship.

Alone on the Edge of Her Competence

While it is true that the average man makes more money than the average women, one-third of U.S. households have a woman who makes more money than her male partner. This can be a source of shame for the man, not because the woman in his life is shaming or critical of his ability to make a living but because the picture in his head—and in the heads of his male peers—is the old, traditional model that says the man is the primary breadwinner and should make more money. This puts them both in a bind: The more she excels, the worse he feels. His resentment, caused not by her success but by his own shame, will drive them irrevocably apart.

Alone, Period

When any of these voids exist in a woman's life, it leaves a hole in her heart—a space waiting to be filled by someone or something to ease the pain of isolation. Sometimes the void can be filled with girlfriends, children, work, or hobbies—but the substitutes will not suffice forever. Of course, all this will increase his sense of failure. The good news is that a man can change this in very simple ways that do not include "talking about the relationship." Here are a few examples:

ALONE AT HOME

- Acknowledge that it is your responsibility, as well as hers, to keep your home life functioning satisfactorily.
- Appreciate all that she does for the home and family.
- Do your share of household chores, management, and meal preparation—make it less of a division of labor and more of a together activity.
- Do the chores you agreed to in a timely fashion.
- Notice what needs to be done and do it *without* being told, asked, or reminded.
- Willingly pay for help maintaining the residence.
- Notice when she makes home improvements.
- Pick up after yourself, and pick up after others.

ALONE IN HER DREAMS

- If you know her dreams, keep them in mind when you make decisions.
- If you don't know her dreams, pay attention and let her teach you.
- Understand that her dreams change—you need to continually update your information.
- Understand that her dreams are not the same as yours.
- Understand you have the ability to make her extremely happy.
- Understand you have the ability to make her extremely unhappy.
- Become the guardian of her dreams, and make fulfilling and honoring them a priority.
- Take pleasure in fulfilling and honoring her dreams.

ALONE ON THE OUTSIDE OF HIS LIFE

- Suggest and plan activities that include her.
- Make sure that each week includes activities you enjoy together.
- Pay attention to her when you are out in public together.
- Develop rituals for time at home that include her, for example, drinking coffee together in the morning, cooking dinner together, watching birds together.
- Increase contact time with her—affectionate touching or shared activities when work hours get long.

ALONE IN BED

- Pay attention to her when sex isn't the motivation.
- Let her know she's beautiful, attractive, sexy, sensual, not as a form of foreplay. If you can't tell her with your smile, send her a note, e-mail, or text message.
- Pay attention to her sexual needs and notice if she's satisfied or not.
- Accept that her sexual needs are different from yours.
- Become an expert in arousing her intimately and sexually.
- Understand that she wants a great sex life.
- Do what you need to do to be a great sex partner.

ALONE ON THE EDGE OF HIS DEPRESSION

- Understand that depression often shows up as alcoholism, drug addiction, anger, irritability, anxiety, obsessive thoughts, controlling behavior, excessive guilt, insecurity, apathy, withdrawal, lack of motivation, procrastination, low sexual desire, and/or compulsive behaviors such as overeating, watching or reading pornography, having affairs, flirting, shopping, spending, and using the computer constantly. If you have one parent who had any of these behaviors, there is a 50 percent chance you will be depressed. If you have two parents with these behaviors, there is a 75 percent chance you will be depressed.
- Acknowledge any symptoms of depression you might have.

- Utilize the many resources available to offset depression, such as books, tapes, Internet sites, medical advice, or professional mental health support. You might be surprised at how many other men suffer like you do. A good buddy can be an outstanding resource.
- Understand that depression is highly treatable and that taking steps to alleviate the symptoms will go a long, long way toward improving your relationship without talking!

ALONE IN HER FEARS

- Don't go there—with your anger, that is. The angrier you are, the scarier you are. The best way to get over being a scary person to the woman in your life is to control your anger. Contrary to popular belief, suppressing your anger will not make you depressed. Therapists used to think that depression was anger turned inward, but now we know that more often, *anger is depression turned outward*. You *can* transform your anger. Do it. If you can't do it alone—get help. It can be done.
- It should go without saying that chronic resentment, angry outbursts, verbal aggression, emotional abuse, and physical violence have no place in relationships. If any of these behaviors have been a part of your life, run—don't walk—to the bookstore for Steven's book *You Don't Have to Take It Anymore: Turn Your Resentful, Angry, or Emotionally Abusive Relationship into a Compassionate, Loving One*. It is hands-down the very best resource for eliminating destructive behaviors that leave women alone in their fears.

ALONE ON THE EDGE OF HER COMPETENCE

- A man must see his role as protector and provider as more than just bringing home money. He has to protect and provide the emotional well-being of his loved ones. It's important to keep in mind that the more competent she becomes, the more responsibility she has on her shoulders and the more she needs him to support and protect her. Every man knows what goes with accomplishment: lots of expectations and responsibilities. That burden can only be lightened by love and connection with a partner.

ALONE, PERIOD

▾ Women want men in their lives. They don't want to be driven away. They want to be in a relationship and experience the benefits that love offers just as men do, which explains why following any of the guidelines put forth in this book can greatly improve your relationship without talking.

If you are a woman and find yourself eager to get the man in your life to read this chapter—STOP! Before you can expect him to make any changes, you have to model the behavior yourself. Let *your* new, improved behavior speak for the efficacy of this book and only then can you share this chapter with him. Even if he never reads it, you can still improve your relationship without talking about it.

If you're a man reading this chapter, it is intended to make you feel compassionate, not guilty! Most of the negative consequences of the behaviors described in this chapter are unintentional, but they have the effect of hurting your partner and keeping you isolated from the most important person in your life. We will show you how to reverse these behaviors in Part II, after one last warning of what can happen if you do not.

how fear and shame lead to infidelity, separation, and divorce

nicole's alarm clock blares for seven minutes before she slaps the snooze button and rolls over with a groan. She can't remember the last time she had more than six hours of sleep in a night. After another snooze she finally pries open an eye to peek at the time. A rush of adrenaline surges through her body like an electrical shock—she's overslept again! Here goes another day of running two steps behind.

Despite the late start, she manages to quell the morning chaos and get herself and three kids ready for the day. She kisses her husband, Raphael, and grabs a bagel as she dashes out the door. The two of them haven't shared more than thirty consecutive minutes alone together in months other than to discuss finances, exchange schedules, and decide who is going to shuttle the kids to their soccer practices, piano lessons, gymnastics classes, social activities, and school events.

On the way to the office Nicole calls her work voice mail to get a head start on the day. She used to spend commute time catching up with friends or listening to her favorite CDs, but now she starts working on the way to work. Yet even with the hectic schedule she's glad she made the decision to go back to work. The extra income helps pay for the latest fashions, newest high-tech gadgets, and other must-haves as dictated by the children.

From the minute she walks into the office, it's nonstop phone calls and meetings. Despite the frenzied pace and never-ending demands, her work buddies make time to break away for an off-site lunch. As usual, lunchtime is comic relief from the uptight professionalism at the office. Today two coworkers argue playfully over whose spouse has the worst personal hygiene habit. Nicole laughs to herself, realizing how much private information she knows about her coworkers. The fact is, she spends more time with them than with her own husband, family, or friends. She hasn't seen her brother and sister for over two years. She had to miss her best friend's birthday party because of a work deadline. She has a closet full of partially completed projects ranging from scrapbooking to oil painting. She goes to worship services, but her mind races with thoughts of chores left undone at home. She's the epitome of the ideal fitness club member: pay the monthly fee, work out diligently for about two weeks, and then never go again. They took a family vacation last year, but this year she had to use her time off just trying to stay on top of life's daily demands. She and Raphael haven't had sex in weeks, not even a romantic kiss or a hug that lasted more than two seconds. Every time she tries to make time for a real conversation with him, she feels like she's talking to a stone wall. She can't remember the last time anyone paid exclusive attention to her for more than ten minutes. Her daily pleasure consists of indulging in a bowl of ice cream as she zones out watching TiVo recordings of *Oprah* and *Trading Spaces*.

Sound familiar? We hope not, because Nicole's life represents a lack of connection to herself and the people she loves. Her life is so stressful that her relationships have become barely workable. Because this superhectic lifestyle happened gradually, she doesn't even think of it as anything but normal; her only focus is survival. If you are living a life like this—one that only works when you catch every light green—intimate connection, the lifeblood of relationships, will be difficult if not impossible.

Who is to say which came first: her busyness or her husband's withdrawal? They usually happen simultaneously. Because a relationship doesn't cry out, demand, or e-mail, it is very easy to put it on the back burner. Nicole cannot go on in this deprived state indefinitely—her soul needs nourishment. Unbeknownst to her, she is a sitting duck, waiting for the first quick fix that comes her way. In her case, the quick fix had a name—Donald, the project manager assigned to her group.

It began innocently enough with routine office conversation. Then they teamed up to work on a special project, which led to working lunches that eventually extended past the project deadline. Soon, Donald and Nicole were eating lunch together every day in the company cafeteria. Conversation shifted from work to more personal issues. As they shared intimate details of their lives, their fondness grew. Lunchtime became the highlight of the day for each of them. With Donald in her life, Nicole found a new source of energy. She could go with less sleep, her outlook was rosy, and she lost five pounds in a little over a month. Her coworkers said she seemed happier and even her husband noticed a new sense of confidence. Only Claire, her colleague at work, took a more guarded stance.

"What's with you and Donald?" she asked abruptly one day.

Nicole's face flushed and she became defensive. "Nothing. What do you mean?"

"You're always together. It doesn't look good," Claire responded matter-of-factly.

Though Claire was not her closest friend at work, Nicole had always respected her fairness. "I don't know what you are talking about—we're just friends," Nicole replied.

"Okay," Claire said, dropping the subject. She wasn't the type to interfere.

From this time forward Nicole and Donald ate lunch off site. They made it a point to seek out places that were not frequented by their coworkers, professing that they didn't want others to get the wrong impression.

Nicole felt a closeness she hadn't felt in years. The tragedy of this situation is that Nicole had felt these same feelings for Raphael in the beginning of her marriage. But now she's blinded by one of the most extreme forms of distorted vision: **infatuation.** In this altered state of consciousness you are totally focused on what feels good to you outside the relationship, with little or no regard for your partner. In fact, when Nicole started to feel the high of infatuation with Donald, out of her guilt she began to find fault with her husband—which assuaged her guilt at least momentarily. The more she told herself that Raphael wasn't meeting her needs, the more she felt justified in pursuing the relationship with Donald. By the time she began justifying, Nicole was already in over her head. Her situation would get worse before it got better. Infatuation, like other compulsive behaviors, almost invariably escalates. In order to keep the natural high flowing, you have to have more contact and take more risks.

It will come as no surprise that Nicole and Donald's relationship became an affair. Conversations during their lunches became more romantic. Then lunch was extended into the afternoon parked in Nicole's car. Finally, they consummated their affair on an overnight business trip. Their lying increased, and the quality of Nicole's marriage went down the tubes.

Few would deny the destruction an affair has on a relationship, but exactly when an affair becomes an affair is not so apparent. Shirley P. Glass, in her book *NOT "Just Friends,"* made it very clear: Chemistry plus exclusivity equals an affair. If you are spending time alone with someone you are attracted to for the sole purpose of getting to know this person or because it is enjoyable, you are playing with fire. Privacy allows for intimate conversation and activities that otherwise would be limited. One tip-off that you are starting down the slippery slope is a desire not to let your spouse know how much you think about this fascinating individual.

Infatuation is an altered state of consciousness. Helen Fisher and her colleagues decided to study the brain activity of people under the influence of infatuation.* Here's what they found. When the subject focused on the loved one, little or no blood went to the neocortex—the rational, reality-testing part of the brain. When you are under the spell of chemistry, you *cannot* think rationally. This stimulating vacation from mundane reality testing is no small part of what we really like about infatuation. But it's important to realize that you are not in your right mind!

Why We Love: The Nature and Chemistry of Romantic Love, by Helen Fisher.

Chemistry is mainly a function of your DNA.* It has more to do with metabolism than personality or values. Now here's the real kicker. The chemical bath your brain enjoys during infatuation is a powerful regulator of fear and shame. Under normal circumstances, Nicole's fear and Donald's shame would have inhibited their attraction to each other. But once they allowed their emotions to attune to each other under the cover of privacy, the inhibitory power of their fear and shame vanished. This sharp reduction of the influence of fear and shame is why, when infatuated, you feel so confident and proud while doing things that you might otherwise find fear-invoking or shameful. One reason that affairs rarely turn into viable relationships when they break up marriages is that the chemical relief from fear and shame is short-lived. (The divorce rate for affair partners who marry is 80 percent!) Once the narcotic effects of infatuation wear off, the woman is likely to feel more insecure and the man more ashamed of himself than ever.

But initially the fear and shame dynamic is harshest on the wronged partner. The anxiety of a woman whose husband has even an emotional connection to another woman goes through the roof, while the humiliation of a cuckolded husband in the past has been culturally sanctioned as an excuse for domestic violence and even murder. Fear of isolation and deprivation also explain why a woman will seldom ask for a divorce when her husband has an affair, while men are highly likely to find the marriage intolerable after their wives have strayed.

Chemistry Is Everywhere

If you meet enough people, you will certainly find someone with whom you feel chemistry. It doesn't matter if you are happily married and securely attached—if you spend private or secret time with someone you're attracted to, the chemistry will escalate into infatuation. Along with your natural in-

*For more information on the relationship between DNA and the chemistry of infatuation, refer to *The Truth About Love: The Highs, the Lows, and How You Can Make It Last Forever,* by Pat Love.

hibitions of fear and shame, your rational decision making will go out the window—you'll be calling him your soul mate when you've never had a real date in public let alone weathered a disappointment. Because you cannot avoid the trap of chemistry, it is absolutely crucial to be honest with yourself about your commitment to your relationship and the ground rules that you both agree upon. The following quiz can help.

Strength of Commitment Quiz

The following items represent beliefs and practices related to the strength of your commitment to your partner and your relationship. Read each statement and answer "true" or "false."

1. I focus more on my partner's faults than on his/her strengths. _____

2. I have habits of great concern to my partner (for example, drinking, spending, overworking, flirting, displaying anger). _____

3. I am in a better mood at work than I am at home. _____

4. I am difficult to live with. _____

5. I prefer sharing exciting events with someone other than my partner. _____

6. I put my own needs before my partner's. _____

7. I put my own needs before the needs of the relationship. _____

8. I wouldn't want my partner to know about all the activities I engage in on the computer. _____

9. I have romantic fantasies about a person in my life other than my partner. _____

10. I dress to attract the attention of someone other than my partner. _____

11. I talk negatively about my partner to others. _____

12. I would rather spend time with my friends/colleagues than my partner. _____

13. I have romantic feelings for someone other than my partner. _____

14. I have sent e-mails I would not want my partner to read. _____

15. I get more pleasure from work than from my relationship. _____

16. I have more than one friend that I am closer to than my partner. _____

17. I put far more energy into work than into my relationship. _____

18. I'm nicer to other people than I am to my partner. _____

19. There is someone who brightens my mood far more than my partner. _____

20. It feels like my partner and I are growing apart. _____

21. I am frequently in a bad mood. _____

22. I get more pleasure from e-mail relationships than from my relationship with my partner. _____

23. Much of the time I spend with my partner I am stressed out or exhausted. _____

24. I am continually multitasking. _____

25. It's difficult for my partner to get my undivided attention. _____

26. I give my hobbies/pastimes more attention than I give my partner. _____

27. My favorite activities do not include my partner. _____

28. I leave it up to my partner to keep the excitement going. _____

29. My life has few high points. _____

30. Even good events don't make me as happy as I think they should. _____

Total of "true" answers _____

The purpose of this quiz is to give you an objective look at your commitment to your relationship—as well as your general well-being. It is important to remember that your overall attitude reflects the strength of your commitment to a happy, healthy relationship. Generally, the more "true" answers you gave, the weaker your commitment.

If you do not consistently shine the light of your soul on your relationship, it can die without your ever talking about it.

Other Forms of Deprivation

Looking back at Nicole's life, you can see that she had emotionally vacated her marriage long before she met Donald, and by all indications her husband, Raphael, had done the same. Here are some clues to how the life was drained from their relationship.

- Kids involved in too many activities. **Research shows that involving children in more than two activities per week can put undue stress upon the child as well as upon the family. Nicole and Raphael could have carved out a significant chunk of quality family and/or couple time by limiting the children's weekly activities.**

- Overinvolved with work. **Nicole started working before she got to work. Most jobs are never finished; you just have to quit at the end of the day and the next day pick up where you left off. She could have used the time on the way to work to make friendly contact with Raphael, and she could have had lunch with him on occasion instead of always opting to go to lunch with coworkers. Or she could have invited him to lunch with her coworkers on occasion, which is a great idea because they would become what Shirley Glass calls "friends of the marriage."**

- Consumer spending. **If the children are dictating purchases for the latest fashions, newest high-tech gadgets, and other must-haves, this could be another indication of a never-ending work-and-spend cycle that deprives relationships of life-giving energy.**

- Addicted to the intensity. **Nicole's daily schedule begs the question of whether she is addicted to intensity. It's easy to become dependent on the high you get from living life in the fast lane, because it temporarily relieves the discomfort of fear and shame. The problem is** that stress increases self-centeredness and disconnection, both of which eventually increase fear and shame.

- Ignoring family and friends. Family and friends serve a vital function for relationships. It's very likely that Nicole's brother, sister, and best friend were standing by when she married Raphael. In this way, they not only hold Nicole's history but also hold the history of her relationship. While new friends are great, there's nothing like old friends and family members to remind us of who we are and where our commitments lie.

- Ignoring enriching activities. Hobbies, cultural activities, and entertainment all serve a purpose in one's life. When you ignore these sources of vitality, you leave a void where unwanted activities can become far too important. Enriching activities can also infuse a relationship with energy when enjoyed together.

- Spiritual neglect: There, but not there. It's clear by the fact that Nicole attends worship services that spirituality had an important place in her life at one time. Having standards to uphold keeps us grounded in what we believe and reminds us of our values and commitments. Attending worship services with your partner and/or family is an important way to strengthen these relationships.

- No physical exercise. It is impossible to feel your best when you neglect your body. Nicole and Raphael could easily have made physical activities a part of their marital and/or family relationship. Another missed opportunity.

- No sex. When a couple abstains from sex, they leave a gaping hole in their relationship. If you don't believe this, check out Chapter 10!

- No romance. Romance is one of the primary reasons two people get together. Romance is tangible proof that you are special, that you are loved, that your partner is attracted to you. When romance fades, interest does too. And just think what an important message it would send to their children if Nicole and Raphael were romantic with each other.

- No exclusive attention, no demand for attention. Not only was there a paucity of exclusive attention between Nicole and Raphael, but also neither of them was demanding it! Your commitment to your relationship requires that you not let your partner ignore you.

♥ Zoning out with ice cream and TV. There's nothing wrong with ice cream or TV, but when it's your only source of pleasure it reinforces distance and keeps love at bay.

Nicole's life may or may not sound extreme to you, but we wanted to make an important point with her story. When you are living life in the fast lane, devoid of enriching activities and quality time with the people you say you love, you are forcing yourself to see life through monocular vision, which is highly self-centered and destructive to your relationship. Self-centeredness is the antithesis of love, for you only *feel* love when you are *loving*. If we had confronted Nicole earlier in the story about being more loving to Raphael, she would likely have told us how busy she was and how little discretionary time she had. But the truth is, she made time for Donald. The opposite of love is not hate—it's indifference.

How indifferent are you to your relationship?

Throughout Part I of the book we have explained how your relationship can begin to fail with neither of you doing anything wrong, if you do not understand the extent to which fear and shame disconnect you from each other. This disconnection is so uncomfortable that it often leads to living separate lives under the same roof, to infidelity, and ultimately to divorce. But there is also a great deal of hope in the discomfort and pain of disconnection—it means that you still *want* to be connected and that you still love each other. The rest of the book will show you how to deepen and fortify your connection and make it as powerful and as valuable as you both want it to be.

using your fear and shame to create love beyond words

seven

your core values

You have learned numerous ways to avoid fear and shame since tod-dlerhood. Though many of your avoidance strategies can work well in most areas of your life, they will eventually disconnect you from your partner and make you feel isolated in your relationship. The problem is that they've become so habitual over the years that it will seem awkward to you when you first start learning new patterns of behavior. There is only one path the brain takes to correct old habits and acquire new ones: *practice, practice, practice!* The good news is that most of the effort is in the begin-ning. Once you learn a new skill, your brain starts doing it pretty much on automatic pilot. It will take you quite a bit of practice to gain a love beyond words, but once you master the skills, you will do them reflexively, without stopping to think about it.

One thing is certain: You won't learn anything by beating yourself up or condemning your partner when either of you makes a mistake. We will stress two things in Part II of this book: self-compassion and compassion for your partner. Compassion for yourself means understanding how diffi-cult it is to change old patterns and how much you *deserve* to change them to get the kind of relationship you've always wanted. Compassion for your partner means understanding how difficult it is for him or her to change old patterns and how deserving he or she is to have a closer relationship with you.

To help you appreciate how awkward it can be to change old patterns, try this experiment. Hold your hands out in front of you and then clasp them together, fingers interlocking. Look at your hands and notice which thumb is on top and which pinkie is on the bottom. Now unclasp them and clasp them together again, with the opposite thumb on top and opposite pinkie on bottom. You probably noticed how awkward this feels. If changing such a trivial habit like this feels awkward, you can imagine how changing the way you interact with your partner on a routine basis will feel. *Don't let the initial awkwardness stop you.* It *has* to feel awkward at first—that's what changing habits is all about! But it will become more natural the more you do it.

The Best Place to Start

The best place to start changing old patterns and begin realizing your enormous power to strengthen your relationship is to write out your answer to the following question.

What is the most *important thing about you as a person?*

There are a lot of important things about you; we want you to write down the *most* important. You would be a different person without this quality. Note: Some people cite important qualities like honesty or loyalty. These are certainly important qualities but not the *most* important. Think of how you would like your children to describe you when they are adults. Would you like them to say the following? "We always knew that Mom and Dad were honest; we're not sure that they always loved us, but we know that they were always honest." Or would you rather they say this? "Mom and Dad were human and made a few mistakes, but I always knew that they loved us."

Now write answers to the following questions:

What is the most important thing about you as a partner?

What is the most important thing about your life in general?

In their answers to the questions above, we have never had a man write that the most important thing about him is his shutting down emotionally, ignoring, resenting, or devaluing the woman in his life. And no woman has ever written that the most important thing about her is criticizing, nagging, or shaming her partner. No men or women have ever written that they always have to be right or have the last word or win the argument. The overwhelming majority of men and women in love relationships write something like the following:

The most important thing about me as a person and partner is my love, protection, and support of my family.

It's not always direct, though, and maybe it wasn't for you. Sometimes we have to "work the whys" to get to the person's most important thing. For instance, many men will say that their intelligence is the most important thing about them.

So we ask, "*Why* is that important to you?"

He'll typically say, "Because I can get a better job."

"*Why* is that important to you?"

"It makes me successful."

"*Why* is that important to you?"

"Because I can provide for my family better."

Sometimes women will write something like "Knowledge that my family cares about me" as the most important thing about them.

"*Why* is that important to you?" we ask.

"Because it will be safer to care about them," they usually say. Almost invariably it comes down to caring for the people you love.

Although there is more variation in answers to the third question, on the most important thing about their lives in general, most people write something along the lines of: *Making the world a better place, at least in some small way, for someone else—family, community, country, humanity, nature, or God.*

Here's the crucial point regarding the most important things about you as a person and as a partner. **Every time you violate your core values** (what you have written)—**even if you're just reacting to your partner—you feel guilty.** For example, if one of your core values is to be a loving partner and you forget your anniversary, you'll feel guilty. Guilt is the direct result of your beliefs and actions being out of alignment with each other. It's your brain's way of warning you to get back in line with your core values. If you're a woman, guilt stimulates a deeper, unconscious fear of isolation, deprivation, or harm. "If I'm not a loving partner, he won't love me and I will be left alone." If you're a man, it taps into your deepest sense of failure as a partner and protector. Whether you're a man or woman, going against your values causes a state of tension in your body and in your psyche. The only way back to a calm and peaceful state is to be true to yourself, which means being true to your deepest values.

The easiest way to keep true to your core values is to invoke what we call the four core value inspirations:

IMPROVE

APPRECIATE

CONNECT

PROTECT

Inspiration means "breathe in." If you take a deep breath and try to improve, appreciate, connect, or protect, you will find yourself back to what is most important to you. You will no longer want to attack, devalue, or defend yourself; you will want to improve, appreciate, connect, and protect. Each inspiration by itself will lead you back to connection with your partner; doing all four together will make you feel euphoric. Here's how they work:

When you inspire yourself to *improve,* you try to make things just a *little* better—1 percent will do to start. Thanks to the powerful human inspiration to improve, you don't necessarily have to "fix" the problem to feel better. You just have to make it a *little* better. If you're feeling bad and you think about what you can do to make it a little better—you don't even have to *do* it, just *think* of it—you'll start feeling better. If you're upset at your partner, and you think of how you can make yourself feel a little better— shower, take a walk, smell a flower, call a friend, watch a game, chop some firewood, read a book—you'll start to feel better. Making things a *little* better frees more mental resources in the neocortex, the problem-solving part of the brain. These added mental resources allow you to make things *even* better, freeing up more mental resources that enable you to improve yet a little more, and so on. Even if the improvement is only in your head, it will change your emotional demeanor and that will make negotiations with your partner go much better.

Think of something you feel guilty or resentful about right now. Think of it in detail. Now think of what you can do to improve either the situation or your experience of it just a little. For instance, Steven right now feels guilty for not returning his dear friend's phone call. At first he thought he was resentful because she left a message when she knew he had to work on the book this morning. But it was really guilt for violating his core value about caring how she feels. He *improved* his experience of the situation by promising himself that he would call at the first opportunity and apologize for not calling sooner.

Appreciate means to value your partner. Appreciation, in turn, makes *you* feel more alert and alive; you increase the value of your *own* life when you appreciate your partner in any way. When your partner feels your appreciation, you don't have to worry about whether you compliment or praise him or her enough. And if you felt your partner's appreciation, you wouldn't feel so bad that he or she doesn't think to compliment you. As a matter of fact, compliments seem empty if they do not convey in some sense that your life is better at this moment because of the person you appreciate.

Think of something you feel guilty (or resentful) about right now, then think of something you can appreciate about the person stimulating the guilt. In Steven's example, he appreciated that his friend was probably concerned about his working under the stress of a deadline. What started out as resentment about her "thoughtlessness and encroachment on his writing time" turned into appreciation of her thought*ful*ness. And even if that were not the case this time, he appreciated that she is usually thoughtful.

To *connect* means to genuinely care about your partner's emotional state. Intimate connection is a sense that your emotional world is an important part of your partner's. Connecting requires at least an intuitive understanding of his shame and her fear, along with the knowledge that your emotional well-being is tied up together—if he feels good, you feel good; if she feels bad, so do you.

Think of something you feel guilty (or resentful) about right now, then think of how you can connect with the person stimulating the guilt. In Steven's example, he took just a second from his writing to think of how he will enjoy talking to his friend when he gets a chance. Needless to say, his eventual conversation will go much more pleasantly with that attitude than if he continued to resent her for calling when he was busy.

Protecting your partner is helping *him* relieve his dread of failure as a provider, lover, protector, and father and helping *her* relieve her fear of isolation, deprivation, and harm.

Think of something you feel guilty (or resentful) about right now, then think of how you can *protect* the person stimulating the guilt. In Steven's example, he thought of how he will make his friend feel valued when they talk, which will reduce her anxiety.

Improving, appreciating, connecting, and protecting create closer connection. The opposite of devaluing, they are powerful weapons against reactivity. Here's an example of the four inspirations in action.

Maria was fed up with Toby's giving her the cold shoulder. Sometimes she thought that he could easily spend the rest of his life sulking on the sofa. Her usual reaction was to try to make conversation, but her efforts typically yielded only one-word responses. Eventually she'd confront him about his coldness, which, of course, he would deny, implying that she was too sensitive or too demanding. But this time, after attending one of our seminars, Maria tried to think of what she could do to make *herself* feel better. She got out their wedding pictures. Just the thought of doing this made her feel more than a *little* better; as she paged through the album, she started to feel *happy*. She felt so good that she shared the pictures with Toby. Her genuine warmth about the pictures—very different from nagging him about his coldness—warmed *him* up, and he too enjoyed the photos. Before they were finished, he apologized for his sulking—the same sulking he had vigorously denied.

It's important to note that they would not have connected in this way had Maria tried to think of a way to bring Toby around. Then she would have come off as manipulative. Sharing the pictures worked to warm up Toby *only* because it had genuinely warmed up Maria; he merely reacted to her warmth. The change had to occur in Maria first. Her intention was to make herself feel a little better, not share the pictures with Toby. Once her core value was activated—she became the person she most wants to be—she naturally chose to *connect* with her husband by sharing the pictures with him and thereby became the life partner she most wants to be.

The real shift in Maria came less from the photos than from her inspiration to *improve*. She would have felt better looking at the pictures—or anything else she valued—whether or not she also chose to *appreciate* her relationship, *connect* with Toby, and *protect* him from his self-destructive sulking. And she would have felt better acting on her inspiration to improve even if Toby had chosen to go on sulking after she brought him the photos. **She would not have allowed his resentful behavior to control her core**

values. That's why the inspiration to improve is a no-lose venture, even if it does not always bring about connection.

Now answer the "most important" questions again, this time with how you think your partner would answer for him/herself.

What do think your partner thinks is the most *important thing about him or her as a person?*

What do you think your partner thinks is the most *important thing about him or her as a partner?*

What do you think your partner thinks is the most *important thing about his or her life in general?*

If you're unsure how your partner might respond to these questions, don't worry. The rest of this book will help you get close enough to know each other's core values, which will almost certainly strengthen the connection between you, without having to talk about it. To get an idea of how knowing each other's core values can bring you closer, consider the following examples:

- ♥ Jaclyn knows that providing for their family is the most important thing to her husband. He didn't have to tell her this; she knew it by his tension about work and the bills. She gladly took some of the financial pressure off him by agreeing to drive their old car one more year, even though she wanted a new one.
- ♥ Gene has stopped trying to influence how much time Melinda

spends in church activities. He never got it when Melinda told him—repeatedly—that her volunteer work in the church was important to her. But one day he went with her to distribute food to the elderly and observed firsthand her animation and sense of purpose. Although he still wasn't wild about her frequent absences from the house to do church activities, he transformed his resentment into respect and admiration.

* Trudy knows that being a good father is important to Sam. Instead of nagging him about spending more time with the kids, she offered to cover for him in their business so he could coach his daughter's softball team. Trudy's been overjoyed watching Sam's excitement and experiencing the benefits of his good mood and closeness with his daughter.

We cannot say enough about the importance of staying true to your deepest values and of honoring those of your partner. If you make this a regular practice, your relationship will not only improve but also be transformed without your ever talking about it.

The capacity to stay true to your deepest values—and thereby transform most of your fear and shame—lies entirely *within* you. If you remain true to your answers to the "most important" questions, you will most likely have a strong connection with your partner. And in the end, you will judge yourself by *your own* efforts and behavior, not by your partner's. On your deathbed, you won't regret what he/she did or did not do; you'll think about *your* fidelity to the most important things about you. When you are upset, angry, or resentful, try to focus less on what your partner is doing and ask yourself these questions:

Am I acting like the person I most want to be? If not, what can I do to act like that person? Answer: Improve (make it a little better), appreciate, connect, or protect.

Am I being the partner I want to be? If not, what can I do to be that kind of partner? Answer: Improve (make it a little better), appreciate, connect, or protect.

Remaining true to your core values, regardless of what your partner does, is the necessary first step in relationship improvement. The next step is to deepen your understanding of your partner's perspective, which means learning to recognize fear and shame in your relationship.

eight

learning to transform fear and shame in your relationship

You've probably guessed by now that avoiding fear and shame presents a major obstacle to behaving in accordance with your core values. To stay true to your core values, you can't avoid fear and shame, you have to *transform* them. And to improve your relationship, you must transform your fear or shame into compassion for your partner's. That's a tall order. How can you even recognize your partner's vulnerability when wrapped up in your own?

The good news is that your own fear or shame is the most reliable signal that your partner is also feeling vulnerable and that he or she is in need of compassion just as much as you are. That's right, your own fear or shame is a built-in signal of when your partner is feeling hurt, if you'll just recognize it. Once you recognize your partner's vulnerability you'll be able to show compassion, which makes it far more likely that you'll get compassion in return.

The challenge of being sensitive to your partner's fear or shame lies in the fact that these feelings most often are expressed as anger, resentment, criticism, or blame. This means that you must be the most compassionate, understanding, and loving when you least feel like it. It's a skill that really sounds much harder than it is. And the payoff is priceless, not only for the relationship but for your own self-value. Here are the general principles to remember in developing this invaluable skill:

- If you're a woman and you're feeling resentful, angry, anxious, or afraid and your partner's not helping, he is trying to avoid feeling shame. Your anxiety = his sense of inadequacy or failure. Your anxiety is your most reliable signal of his sense of shame.
- If you're a man and you're feeling resentful, angry, sulky, or withdrawn, and your partner's not helping, she is feeling anxious. Your irritation = her fear. Your irritation is your most reliable signal of her fear of isolation or deprivation.

A clear knowledge of this is crucial. If you hurt your partner when he or she is already hurting, you'll just throw gasoline on the fire. **Before you start to deal with the *content* around the hurt—what specifically is triggering the fear or shame—you must find a *nonverbal* way to connect and show that you value each other.** It has to be nonverbal because fear and shame actually drain blood from the neocortex—the language part of the brain. If you try talking, you will either fumble for the right words or, more likely, use the wrong words and express something different from what you mean. For example, you might be asking your partner to value you, but your words will most likely devalue him or her. In addition, if you are a woman feeling anxious or fearful, and then add talking to the equation, his arousal level will be heightened and talking will make things worse, not better. In contrast, making a nonverbal connection will lower the fear-shame reaction in each of you and enable you to deal more effectively with matters at hand.

Here are a few signals of connection that our clients have come up with. Whatever *you* come up with must be mutually agreed upon and work for *both* of you to signal your equal importance to each other:

- A gesture of affection
- A hug
- A hand signal

* An offer of a cold drink or cup of coffee/tea
* A flower petal
* A lit candle
* A small gift
* Helping out

Recognizing that all relationships have periods of disappointment and disconnection, Pat likes to give couples a special wedding present for these times. She wraps a beautiful goblet with the following message:

True love always has ups and downs. How you manage this normal ebb and flow will determine the course of your relationship. This gift is designed to help you through the low times. If and when you find yourself at a distance, at an impasse, in a bad place—no matter who is right or wrong, fill the glass, remember the love you share today, offer it to your partner, and your connection will be restored.

Love and blessings,
Pat

If you notice, each of these reconnecting gestures requires only one person. Even the gift in Pat's example above is just one goblet. If one person makes a genuine gesture of connection, the other partner will feel the impact even if he or she doesn't reciprocate at that moment. (In fact, a man is more likely to feel the impact in the moment but not act on it until later—mostly because it takes longer for men to metabolize the cortisol that accompanies abrupt arousal from their bloodstreams.) However, a gesture like any of the above increases the likelihood that your connection will be restored sooner rather than later. Even if your partner doesn't respond in the preferred manner, making a gesture of connection will connect *you* to your core values— the most important things about you—and raise the compassion level of the relationship. This can have only a long-term positive effect.

When the two of you feel connected, you can easily solve the problem that originally triggered the resentment, anger, anxiety, or shame; and your solution will be consistent with what you indicated were the *most* important things about both of you.

Don't misunderstand: Your nonverbal gestures should not be ways of avoiding the issue—you don't touch her hand to shut her up or stroke his hair to manipulate him into agreeing with you. They must be sincere gestures of reconnection so that you can resolve the issue without invoking each other's fear and shame. They must convey that your connection is more important than whatever you're ashamed of or angry, resentful, or anxious about. If you find yourself resisting the desire to connect in order to indulge the impulse to argue or punish or make your point, or simply because you don't feel like it, go back and read aloud what you wrote down as the most important things about you as a person and a partner.

Emotion Transformation

We're giving you a tall order: Be at your best when your partner is at his or her worst. We acknowledge how difficult this is and promise that it will become easy to implement with practice. First the hard part: When a surge of emotion *feels* like it's hijacking your body and making you react in a nonloving, noncompassionate way, it may feel good to discharge the emotion and react in the moment, even though the lasting effects can be devastating to your relationship and even harmful to your health. To help in this seemingly daunting but highly rewarding task, we offer the skill of *emotion transformation,* a powerful technique to keep you true to the most important things to and about you under stress. When your partner is on the precipice of fear or shame but coming off as angry, critical, irritable, or resentful, practicing emotion transformation will prevent you from falling into the fear-shame trap. That's when the fear in one of you stimulates shame in the other and vice versa. If you transform your emotions to be consistent with your core values, you'll increase the likelihood that your partner will, too. Happily, transforming your emotions to be consistent with your core values is often just a matter of redirecting them. For example, when you feel like giving up, you can transform that troublesome emotion by making a *small* improvement; when you feel like casting blame, redirect to some form of appreciation; when you feel like withdrawing, redirect toward connecting; or when you feel like attacking, redirect to protection.

The key to transforming emotions is first to recognize them—you can't change what you don't see—and second to use them as guardians of your core values.

Emotion transformation is neither avoiding nor venting. It doesn't mean "suppressing it," "keeping the lid on it," "putting up with it," "ignoring it," or "holding it in." If you have ever tried to avoid or hold back an emotion, like controlling your anger by biting your tongue, you know how hard it is. Your hormones, neurotransmitters, and the entire force of your central nervous system are working to discharge the emotion, while you are consciously trying to suppress it. That's like driving with one foot on the gas and the other on the brake—it gets you nowhere fast and can do serious damage. If you've read many magazines or watched TV, you've probably learned that holding in negative emotions—whether you're aware of them or not—is bad for your physical health and psychological well-being. But this *does not* mean that letting them out is good for you either, especially when you express emotions like anger, contempt, and resentment that devalue your partner. The far healthier alternative to holding them in or letting them spew out is *transforming* them.

To transform an emotion is to use it as a positive motivator, the purpose for which it evolved. Your emotional pain and discomfort are not *punishments* inflicted on you; they are *signals* for you to take corrective action. The pain in your bladder tells you to stop what you're doing, take charge of your physical well-being, and go to the bathroom. Likewise, **the pain in your heart tells you that you have to take charge of your emotional well-being.**

Most of the time, taking charge of your emotional well-being in your relationship means reconnecting with your partner. To transform the anger and resentment that drive you apart, you must focus on the vulnerability causing your resentment and anger. Once you recognize your own vulnerability *and* your partner's (if one is fear, the other will most likely be shame), compassion will likely follow. Here's an example of the kind of thing that has occurred to people who learned the skill of emotion transformation at our workshops.

Cindy had worked hard to organize a dozen or so of her girlfriends into forming a book club, which she planned to launch with a fancy luncheon at her house. Her husband, Jake, seeing that she was in a tizzy about the menu for the luncheon, suggested, somewhat irritably, that she have it catered and "stop stressing about it, already!" Cindy's initial reaction was, as you can imagine, resentful irritation. It seemed to her that Jake was not only dismissing the whole project as silly but also dismissing *her* for putting energy into it. He didn't appreciate that fussing about the menu is a way that Cindy expresses her love and care for her girlfriends. She wondered why he couldn't just stay out of things he doesn't understand. Jake acted as if her feelings were a pain in the neck to him. If he truly believed that, their relationship would be in danger. Her anxiety spiked upward. But then she remembered our workshop, which they had just attended, and realized that Jake was merely responding to her anxiety about the luncheon and, in his own way, trying to help. True, he came off as dismissive, but she understood that his defensiveness sprang from feeling helpless when he saw her upset, because he wanted to see her happy.

After taking a few seconds to figure out the fear-shame dynamics of their interaction, she knew what to do. Cindy resisted the temptation to react to Jake's anger with an outburst of her own. She respectfully declined his offer about the catering and asked him to run two errands for the luncheon that would greatly help her. Jake was grateful to be given a way to help calm Cindy down. She empowered him with a way to help her, which transformed her anxiety and his shame at the same time.

Because Cindy understood that the fear-shame dynamic was undermining their exchange, she not only avoided the old "talking about it" tar pit, which would have made things worse, but also used her insight to forge a connection with Jake that diffused the tension between them. The guiding principle is this: **Be sensitive to your partner's fear or shame and he or she will likely respond in kind.**

So how does this complex process become easy? It has a *built-in* reinforcement system. Converting negative emotions to positive ones feels good! Once you make the effort to start doing it, you'll you feel so much better about yourself and your partner that you'll want to keep doing it, until it becomes a habit that runs on automatic pilot—without your having to stop and think about it, much less talk about it.

Overcoming Barriers

Hopefully you are getting the point that sensitivity to your partner's fear and shame is necessary for a really close relationship. Better yet, you probably recall that when you were first in love you had that sensitivity. So what do you suppose is the number one barrier to getting it back?

You probably guessed it: resentment. Years of reacting to each other's hidden fear and shame have taken a toll on your ability to give each other the benefit of the doubt. The good news is that the propensity to resent each other is just a habit. The bad news is that habits aren't so easy to break. But you can do it, as long as you stay tuned in to the most important things to, and about, you. Let's start right now!

Here's the first step in overcoming resentment. Write down the following statements and read them out loud. (We ask you to write them down because they get into your unconscious more quickly that way, and we ask you to read them aloud because you are more committed to them if you do, particularly if you read them aloud in front of another person.)

My emotional well-being is important to me.
My emotional well-being is more important than everything I resent.
My emotional well-being is more important than anyone else's bad behavior.
My relationship is more important than everything I resent and worthy of appreciation, time, energy, effort, and sacrifice.

Think of something that you resent about your partner—for example, his anger, stonewalling, negativity or her nagging, criticism, overspending, withholding sex. Think about how you respond to that behavior, for example, by judging, getting defensive, lashing out, shutting down, or withdrawing. Then ask yourself: Are you being true to the *most* important thing about you as a person and as a partner when you respond that way?

If you answered no, think of what your response would look like if you *were* consistent with the most important things about you as a person and as a partner. Women, you might try to understand his point of view and express compassion for the shame that's making him angry, resentful, or withdrawn. Men, you might try to make a connection with her, rub her shoulders, or lend a hand to relieve her stress. In short, you both would find some way to let the other know that you care, if you were true to the most important things about you as a person and as a partner.

Replacing Resentment with Compassion

Contrary to popular belief, the most important of all attachment emotions is not love, it's *compassion*. Why, you're probably wondering, is compassion more important than love?

Compassion makes us sensitive to the individuality, depth, and vulnerability of loved ones. It makes us appreciate that they are different from us, with a separate set of experiences, a different temperament, and, of course, different vulnerabilities to fear and shame, all of which leads them to give different meanings to the same behaviors. For example, when a woman tells her partner that they "need to talk," she means that she wants to feel closer to him. He *thinks* she wants to tell him yet again that he's failing her. Without compassion, neither of you can understand your differences, even though you certainly love each other.

The very intensity of love, when it exists without high levels of compassion, *seems* to make us merge with each other; we begin to assume that our loved ones see the world exactly the way we do. This obscures what they actually feel, how they think, and, in large part, who they really are. They become merely a source of emotion for us, rather than separate persons in their own right. If they make us feel good, we put them on a pedestal. If they make us feel bad by not seeing the world the way we do, we feel betrayed.

Finally, compassion makes us protective rather than controlling. The difference is crucial. When we're controlling, we want our partners to feel bad for not doing what we want them to do. But when we're protective, we want to help them achieve what is best for them. Most of all, we want them to feel okay about who they are.

If you want your partner to feel compassion for you, you must feel compassion for him or her. If you want him to understand your fear and anxiety, you have to understand his shame, and if you want her to understand your dread of failure, you must understand her anxiety and fear about harm, isolation, and deprivation.

The Highest Form of Compassion

Empathy is a form of compassion that includes identifying with what another person is feeling. "I feel your pain" was a hallmark of empathy, at least before it was lowered to political satire. Empathy is a wonderful thing, but it has limitations in relationships between men and women. Women cannot truly empathize with a man's shame—failure is not so humiliating for her as long as she feels connected; and men cannot truly empathize with a woman's fear—anxiety is not that bad for him as long as he can feel successful. These limitations of empathy often become a trap in intimate relationships:

I can't empathize with you, because I wouldn't be afraid of someone yelling.

I wouldn't be ashamed to ask for a raise, because I wouldn't feel inadequate if the boss said no.

It's relatively easy to have compassion for someone who has lost his sight, because you can close your eyes and imagine how painful it must be to have lost such a precious gift and how hard it would be to learn brand-new skills to get along in a complex environment. But you have a higher form of compassion for a person born without sight, because you cannot imagine what it would be like to have a brain completely lacking in visual imagery. You cannot fathom it, because your brain has developed complex circuitry based on visual imagery. It is beyond your capacity to imagine a world devoid of visual images, which would be like imagining your own death—the closest you can come is thinking about being asleep. Because you cannot "put yourself in the shoes" of the person born sightless, your compassion forces you outside the limitations of your own experience into the world of someone different from you but just as valuable and worthy as you. Your compassion for the person born without sight would naturally include appreciation of your *differences* and admiration for his unique perspectives and greater acuity of other senses. You make yourself a better person by expanding beyond the limitations of your own experience.

This is the kind of compassion we must nurture for each other to make our relationships work. You have different vulnerabilities and can scarcely imagine what it is like to spend your life adapting to your partner's vulnerability. Women need to understand that their partners' vulnerability to shame—and intense avoidance of it—are not quite in their own experience, and men must see that their wives' vulnerability to fear of harm, isolation, and deprivation—and intense avoidance of them—are not quite in the male experience. Couples who achieve this highest form of compassion are *happy* couples. They help each other manage their vulnerabilities rather than hold them against each other.

Don't be daunted by the notion of the "highest compassion"—you've already done it plenty of times without thinking about it. You did it reflexively when you first fell in love. When most women sense the discomfort of their new lovers, they automatically respond with comfort and support, and most men who sense the anxiety of their new lovers automatically respond with connection and protection. In the early days of your love you cared for each other and automatically gave mutual support. As a result, your self-value was at its highest. You felt the best you could feel about yourself because you acted according to your deepest values.

You don't have to relearn compassionate or supportive behaviors. You just have to take the blinders off and let your gut-level sensitivity to each other's subtle dread and fears emerge naturally. Then your own deepest values will take over and you will feel the sheer power of giving comfort and protection to the most important adult in your life.

binocular vision

Why didn't you tell me you were such a hotshot basketball player?" Leticia asked Bo as they were driving home from his high school reunion.

"It wasn't me—it was the team," Bo replied.

"Well, that's not how I heard it. Tyrone and J.J. made it sound like you were the star," Leticia countered.

"I wasn't the star," Bo said softly, hoping to end the conversation.

Leticia pressed on, wanting to know more about this part of her husband's history. "I'll bet it was exciting, winning the championship for the first time."

"Yeah," he replied, still giving no support to her inquiry.

Leticia tried another approach. "What was that like, seeing all those guys again? They were crazy about seeing you."

Bo couldn't help but grin. "They are just crazy, period. Some things never change." Finally, giving in to Leticia's enthusiasm, he began telling the highlights of that winning season. As he talked a flood of feelings rushed over him and his first inclination was to stop, but he pressed on. Leticia laid her head back on the seat and listened intently, picturing the events as Bo let them unfold. Just as he was beginning his third anecdote Leticia's cell phone rang. She thought that perhaps she shouldn't have answered, but ringing phones made her anxious. "Hello. Oh, hi, Howard." It was the nurse practitioner from the clinic who was covering for her while she took time off to attend the reunion; he was calling to make sure he had her schedule right. Leticia finished the call as soon as politeness allowed and then eagerly turned back to her conversation with Bo. "So, start that story again . . ."

"Forget it!" Bo responded angrily.

Leticia froze. "No, I want to hear more . . ." she pleaded.

"No you don't, Leticia."

"What, you can answer your phone, but if I answer mine, I get punished!" Leticia said incredulously.

"Why is it always me punishing you? What about *you* punishing me?" Bo yelled, and then went silent for the rest of the drive.

Leticia was numb. She knew it would do no good to try to pursue the subject further. She also knew the longer they went in silence, the harder it would be to get back to the good connection they were feeling just a few moments ago.

What Happened?

There are many ways to analyze this transaction between Leticia and Bo. She could have ignored the phone; he could have been patient and continued their conversation. Although both of these perspectives have merit, at this time we want to examine only the interaction with the goal of understanding *how* Leticia unintentionally stimulated Bo's shame. As we proceed, it is important to avoid getting caught up in who was right or wrong. **When a woman shames a man, she's wrong even if she's right. When a man stimulates a woman's fear, he's wrong even if he's right.**

Two Different Perspectives

When they first got in the car Leticia was still feeling pride and appreciation in response to the reception Bo had received from his former classmates. He had never talked much about his high school days, and frankly she was taken aback hearing about his outstanding athletic ability as well as seeing the obvious admiration of his buddies. She was looking forward to hearing more about this very attractive side of her husband and taking advantage of the ride home to get more information about his history.

Bo, on the other hand, got in the car feeling the same mixed feelings that had kept him away from the reunions for twenty years. Yes, he remembered the pleasure of setting scoring records in basketball his junior and senior years, but he also remembered the pain of never scoring *socially* in four years. He had been so shy and insecure that, despite his athletic accomplishments, he had lacked the nerve to ask a girl out. So any positive memories of ball games were always tainted by the dreaded postgame ritual of walking out of the gym past groups of girls—all waiting for the *other* guys. Mercifully, the guys didn't give him a hard time about his lack of action—but they didn't have to; he did that himself. It wasn't that he had no interest in girls; he was attracted to many, one in particular, Sarah Jo Bentley. He had a crush on her from the summer of ninth grade until he met Leticia in junior college. When he saw Sarah Jo at the reunion, she was just as pretty and nice as he remembered. Seeing her reminded him of his attraction as well as his shyness, and even though he talked with ease, all he could think of was what a loser he had been in high school.

So Leticia and Bo got in the car with different perspectives and attitudes. She was looking forward to talking at length about Bo's high school history, and all he wanted to do was to forget it. They were each entrenched in their own monocular vision, unaware of the other's perspective. Had either of them been attuned to the other, the scenario would have played out differently.

In the beginning of the conversation, Bo gave several cues indicating that he was not open to a conversation about his high school days. The cues fall into a category known as paralinguistics: above and beyond words. It wasn't simply what Bo said, it's how he said it. Three times he responded to Leticia with an I'm-uncomfortable paralinguistic message. Look at the exchanges:

She said, "Why didn't you tell me you were such a hotshot basketball player?"

He said, "It wasn't me—it was the team."

The fact that he didn't match her enthusiasm was a clue that he wasn't buying into the conversation. Had she been attuned, his non-complementary response would have gotten her attention.

Then she said, "Well, that's not how I heard it. Tyrone and J.J. made it sound like you were the star."

He said, "I wasn't the star." His short answer further confirmed his resistance. He not only rejected the compliment but also took issue with her interpretation.

She persisted: "I'll bet it was exciting, winning the championship for the first time."

He responded, "Yeah." Less than a resounding endorsement for her to continue and further confirmation that he was uneasy.

Then Leticia changed her approach by trying an open-ended question: "What was it like, seeing all those guys again? They were crazy about seeing you."

This approach was far more inviting because it shifted the focus from her to him. Instead of making the observations and waiting for him to comment, she opened the door for him to provide the information with her in the role of listener. Even though Bo responded to this overture, it didn't mean his discomfort had subsided; Leticia's genuine interest simply gave him the courage to open Pandora's box and venture into a topic that still had shame and inadequacy attached to it.

When her phone rang, Leticia responded with monocular vision, entirely from her own frame of reference and clueless to the fact that shifting her focus would leave Bo alone in his vulnerability—that terrible place he had dreaded just moments ago. Insensitive to Bo's earlier warning cues, she answered the phone as if they were having an ordinary conversation that she assumed would be easy to pick up after her phone call. Needless to say, she felt terrible when she realized what she had done.

Again, please understand that the point of this illustration is not to determine who is right or wrong. Shaming Leticia for shaming Bo isn't useful and won't help any of us improve our relationships. We use this true story to make a vital point: Men live on the precipice of shame; women live on the precipice of fear. In order to connect, we must honor and protect each other's respective vulnerabilities. Being attuned to your partner's vulnerability is the first step in seeing his or her perspective.

Let's look at the example from Bo's perspective. Think about it: Here he was, already feeling inadequate from the memory of being ignored by women, then, wham, it happens again! The intensity of his anger reflected the depth of his pain, and a hurt this deep needs a lot of protection. Again, we are not justifying Bo's anger but simply asking you to step into his world for a moment. A world that includes the pain of feeling unworthy of attention and believing you are not good enough to be loved. If you can understand and empathize with Bo's vulnerability, you have taken a step into compassion. Once you have stepped into compassion you have transformed your relationship—without talking.

A Few Practical Facts About Emotions in General and Fear and Shame in Particular

▾ Anything that happens suddenly—positive or negative—increases emotional intensity.

The *sudden* interruption of their conversation by the cell phone gave an extra jolt of adrenaline to Bo. If he'd understood that his spike of arousal was to the suddenness of the phone call and not to Leticia, he might have been disappointed at the timing of the call, but he would not have been angry.

- We are more prone to negative emotions during transitional times—moving from one state to another. That's why we're likely to get irritable leaving the house, driving somewhere, coming back home, and so on. (If you have a toddler, you know well that you are in danger of meltdowns around transitions from play to bedtime, getting ready to go out, in the grocery store, and so on.)

Leticia and Bo would have had an easier evening if they'd understood their increased sensitivity during transitional times. They had left an enjoyable social occasion and were driving home—some lapse into negativity was *likely* to happen. But had they not blamed their transitory negative feelings on each other, these brief, unpleasant feelings would have passed quickly.

- Shame occurs with an abrupt diminishment of interest or enjoyment. This letdown feeling is responsible for many of the irritations of life, like the kind you feel when your interesting or enjoyable phone conversation is interrupted by your friend's call-waiting.

Leticia could have softened the abruptness of the letdown by expressing her own disappointment that her phone rang or simply by touching Bo and saying, "I really want to hear this—let me get rid of this call." Similarly, Bo could have softened his own letdown by thinking of what he would say when Leticia got off the phone.

- Fear of harm, isolation, or deprivation is most likely to occur when emotional connection is broken.

Bo could have helped his shame and Leticia's fear by feeling protective of her anxiety and keeping the mental connection with her while she was on the phone.

Instead, the result was disconnection—and *any* attempt to talk about it while you are disconnected will make it worse. The trick to achieving the kind of connection you want is to develop the advanced relationship skill of *binocular vision,* the artful ability to see your partner's perspective as well as your own.

The Way We Were

There was a time when it was easy to see your partner's perspective. You only have to recall what it was like when you were falling in love. It's unlikely that you completely internalized your partner's point of view while giving up your own, and you probably did not insist that he or she adopt *your* perspective in all important matters. Nor is it completely accurate to say that you both *modified* your perspectives to accommodate each other. Rather, your separate but equal perspectives formed a kind of duet, like a violin and cello playing harmony. The violin doesn't change its perspective to suit the cello and the cello doesn't sell out its cellohood for the sake of the violin. What makes the harmony is the differently pitched strings of the two instruments resonating together, while retaining the beauty of their individuality. You stopped making harmony in your relationship when you tried to criticize or stonewall the violin into becoming the cello and vice versa. Most relationship criticisms and stonewalling take the form of *Why can't you be more like me!* The irony is that you wouldn't have been attracted if your partner was more like you—what could be more boring than living with a carbon copy of yourself? Putting that aside for now, the violin and cello add depth and breadth to each other, and that is precisely what dual perspectives do in a relationship. They do not compete with each other for a single view of reality; they add depth and breadth to your individual pictures of the world.

Another way to appreciate the importance of seeing your partner's point of view without losing your own is to compare monocular with binocular vision. Looking through one eye reduces the area you can see. It also distorts depth perception and lessens your ability to see movement. It's harder to realize this just by covering up one eye because your brain fills in the missing information with guesses of what the other eye would see. It's easier to see the difference using a telescope and pair of binoculars. The development of the latter was a boon to military strategists, though somewhat less fortunate for opposing troops trying to move without being detected. In the wild, it is mostly predatory animals like lions that developed binocular vision—eyes in the front of their heads—that better equip them for seeing movement and judging distances to stalk, chase, and pounce. Prey animals, like deer, who have one eye on either side of their heads, suffer a distinct disadvantage in vision. Although they see better from the side, they cannot judge distance or movement, which they make up for with the size of their herds—what they lack in acuity they make up for in quantity. Besides the obvious fact that they can be killed by predators, part of the reason that prey animals are more nervous and skittish, even in captivity, is that they cannot trust their vision to give them enough information to know when they are safe. Monocular vision enhances anxiety. In human relationships, monocular perspectives breed nervousness, suspicion, and eventually paranoia, which is why you sometimes feel that your partner is out to make your life miserable.

The nice thing about binocular vision is that you don't have to agree with your partner's perspective. The key is to focus on your partner's feelings instead of the facts. You don't have to agree with the facts of your partner's point of view, as long as you give *importance* to the feelings associated with it.

Here's an example: In a conversation, Peter was irritated when he perceived Marci to be criticizing him. There was no way that Marci was going to agree that she *criticized* Peter when she accused him of ignoring her. After all, she made an I statement, like her therapist told her to do. "I feel ignored," she said, hearing her therapist's words in her head. And there was no way Peter would buy into her assessment that he was oversensitive. While they don't have to agree on their interpretations of the facts or even understand each other, they do have to care about how the other feels if they want to stay connected. She really didn't *want* to make him feel criticized and hurt. He didn't *want* to make her feel ignored and unimportant. All they have to do is respond with their gut-level sensitivity to each other's hurt, without defending their alternative perspectives. This is absolutely crucial to create and maintain connection. Binocular vision must include sensitivity to the fear or shame that lies beneath whatever words you use.

Excluding your partner's perspective and insisting on your own, no matter how you put it, implies that being right is more important to you than how your partner feels and more important than the well-being of your relationship.

Adding Dimensions

You will be less able to validate your partner's perspective if it feels like you are *giving* up something to do it. Although it can sometimes feel that way, in truth your partner *cannot* take anything away from your perspective. He or she can only add dimensions to it, which can bring richness and texture to the way you color your world canvas. Here's an example.

Barry did not like his wife's new friend, Jana, whom he saw as self-centered and manipulative. He was certain that she would take advantage of Susan's good heart. Indeed, Susan had been disappointed several times in the past by women who turned out to be more exploitative than supportive. Because Barry sincerely believed that he was trying to look out for Susan's best interest, he was shocked when Susan accused him of being a control freak after he expressed reservations about Jana. Of course, she viewed his criticism of her girlfriend as an attempt to devalue her judgment and control her. Trying to influence behavior without seeing your partner's perspective will always feel possessive and controlling.

By the way, like most marital disputes, this was not a communication problem. Susan and Barry had been to marriage counseling and read half a dozen relationship books—they knew all the "right" things to say. Rather, their problem was a typical failure to appreciate their differences in fear and shame. Susan freely acknowledged that she often chose inappropriate girlfriends, due to her, as she put it, "abandonment issues" (a phrase she got from one of her relationship books). Because Barry didn't have the same fear of isolation, he underestimated it and frequently criticized her for it. Likewise, Susan didn't grasp the sense of inadequacy (failure to protect) Barry felt when he saw her get hurt by her girlfriends. She criticized him for his attempts to *control,* which he perceived as his desire to *protect* her. As long as they each failed at compassion for the other's subtle vulnerabilities and remained stuck in their own perspectives, all the "right things" they'd learned to say in therapy had the wrong effect. Barry only managed to raise Susan's fear of isolation, which *increased* her motivation to reach out to friends with less discrimination than was in her best interest. In other words, the more he criticized her about the friendship, the more she needed the friendship for support. Criticism inevitably drives your partner to someone else in search of support.

Barry's perspective was that Susan needed to overcome her "abandonment issues," which sometimes blinded her to the true character of her girlfriends. If he had validated *her* perspective by using binocular vision, he would have seen the girlfriend through *Susan's* eyes and realized that the woman had some pretty good qualities. He would have also appreciated the sense of value that Susan got from the relationship. He would have enjoyed this *added* dimension to his own perspective without *giving up* his hope that Susan would be cautious, based on her history. In addition, sympathy with her perspective would have lowered Susan's anxiety. Then she could have seen the girlfriend apart from her own fear of isolation. This would have allowed her to make a clear assessment of her girlfriend's character, which would have deepened their relationship or perhaps advised her to withdraw from it. As she learned to appreciate Barry's protectiveness, she was able to appreciate his concern while deciding for herself who her friends would be. This mutual compassion, engendered by binocular vision, would have brought them closer together as a couple.

The Brains of Binocular Vision

When it comes to sight, your brain does a magnificent job of naturally producing binocular vision by integrating information from your left and right eyes. But your brain needs some coaching to develop a similar binocular vision in relationships. The reason we need to *learn* this relationship skill is that the brain is organized in a highly subjective manner. Your view of the world is shaped by your experience and is therefore highly biased toward *your* point of view. Here's a thumbnail sketch of this complex process.

It's fair to say that you are born with a brain but no mind. In other words, the brain comes with some assembly required. The infant brain has billions of receptors, known as neurons, but few circuits connecting them. Neural circuits are formed in response to stimulation from the environment—entering the brain via the senses (sight, hearing, touch, taste, and smell). Stimulation sends an electrical charge through the neurons and jump-starts electrochemical impulses, neurotransmitters. These neurotransmitters leap between neurons and form a neural pathway, which permits the neurons to fire together in the future with speed and ease. Repetitive stimulation strengthens the connections. Neurons that fire together wire together.* Every time a baby learns something new, his or her brain forms neural circuits, or pathways, that create associations and memory. This is how a baby learns to associate comfort, security, and affection with Momma's breast. It's how he or she learns to recognize Daddy's voice. When Daddy keeps showing up with the same deep vocal tones, baby begins to associate Daddy with these sounds. Baby's memory of Dad will include the unique sound of his voice.

The more an association is made, the more it increases the probability that you will make the same association in the future. We all have thousands of different associations and memories based upon our past experiences.

*Hebb's law, as described in Donald Hebb's *The Organization of Behavior* (New York: Wiley, 1949).

For example, when you think of the word *dog*, you might think of your dog, a particular breed of dog, or perhaps a scary encounter with a dog. You *don't* think of an army boot, scissors, or a picture frame. Over the years your brain has come to associate *dog* with a furry canine, not leather footwear, paper cutters, or a wooden square. A well-worn neural circuit becomes a slippery slope that leads your mind quickly down the same path. Here's a visual to help explain this concept.

Picture a fresh pile of dirt. Now imagine that it's starting to rain. The first time rain hits the top of the pile it is free to run in any direction. However, once a path is formed, subsequent water flow will be inclined to follow the same path. Over time, as the path becomes deeper and a rut is formed, it will be very difficult for water to go in any direction except down that same rut. In a similar manner, going down the same neural pathway time and again forms more or less permanent neural connections.* For example, every time you think, even as a throwaway thought, "My husband's a jerk," the more you will be inclined to see him as a jerk in the future. As you repeat this experience, the neural ruts become deeper. Maybe this is why we call it "being in a rut."

Your brain doesn't merely form associations with ideas and behaviors, it also does it with feelings. The first time you grabbed a diet cola when you were tired, your brain made the connection between being tired and getting a lift from the soda. Repeating this act made the connection stronger. If you continue to use diet cola to alleviate fatigue, you will automatically start to crave it when you get the least bit tired. Eventually you won't be aware of your fatigue, just the longing for the diet cola, because your brain has associated feelings of fatigue with alertness, via the diet cola.

Due to the profound effect of experience on neural pathways, monocular vision is shaped by your past. When all you see is your own point of view, it certainly will be contaminated by your prior experiences and thereby limit future growth. When you are viewing the world through

---

*We'd like to acknowledge and thank Pat's son, Jimmy Lutz, for the dirt pile analogy. Our clients have found this visual to be extremely helpful. Thanks, Jimmy!

monocular vision your brain jumps to conclusions. For example, if experience has wired your brain to see women as hard to please, it will be easy to believe the woman in your life is hard to please. If your experience has wired your brain to associate men with being untrustworthy, your inclination will be to see the man in your life as untrustworthy. And that's not the worst of it—the more negative experiences you have in your history, the more your monocular vision will create anxiety and suspicion. Here's a true story to illustrate this point.

At age nineteen, Diana married a man who turned out to be repeatedly unfaithful. The years she spent living with lies and betrayal created many negative impressions of men. Finally she got the courage to leave the marriage; unfortunately she took the hurts and negative associations with her. Years after her divorce she was still highly suspicious of men, and it seemed like every man she met had a history of infidelity—even if he wouldn't "admit it." Finally, after numerous disappointments and failed relationships, she went into therapy. Through sometimes painful self-examinations she began to understand how her history had wired her brain to see men as untrustworthy, and, more important, how her fear was keeping her from creating a happy love relationship. Three years later she met Brandon and after a long, cautious courtship they decided to marry. But before she would move in with him, Diana asked that he grant her one wish: to go through his house and remove all the symbols of his bachelor life. She did not want to be confronted with reminders of his former relationships. She didn't ask him to destroy any items, just simply to put them away where she wouldn't see them. Brandon readily agreed. He promptly purged his house of pictures, mementos, letters, and any paraphernalia associated with his single life. Diana moved in and everything went swimmingly until one day while Brandon was at work, she opened a drawer in the bathroom and found a plentiful supply of condoms. (She had had a hysterectomy. He had a vasectomy. They were both HIV negative, and they had been monogamous for over a year. Therefore they didn't use condoms.) After the discovery in the bathroom, it seemed everywhere she looked there were condoms—in the bedroom, in the closet, even in the dining room!

That evening when Brandon came home from work Diana used one of the communication skills she had learned in therapy. She sat down with him and explained how she felt and what she was requesting of him. She used all the *right terms,* such as "I feel . . ." and "What I would like is . . ." Knowing her history, Brandon immediately understood how painful it must have been for Diana to find the condoms. He was very apologetic and told her he would immediately get rid of the condoms. But a couple of days later, as Diana was opening a drawer in the kitchen she looked down, and saw *another condom!*

This time when Brandon came home from work, the communication skills went out the window. As soon as he walked in the door she went to him and slammed the condom down on the table and screamed, "Why did you lie to me! You said you would get rid of the condoms. Why can't I trust you? Don't you care how much this hurts me?"

Brandon turned white. He looked down at the table, then back at Diana, then found within himself the capacity to speak with compassion, "Yes, honey, I do care how much it hurts you—*but that's a tea bag.*"

Diana and Brandon laugh about this incident now because years of positive experiences have replaced their old monocular vision with a much friendlier binocular vision of each other. But before we move on, let's use the condom example to illustrate another concept from neuroscience that explains why it takes effort to change monocular vision to binocular vision.

Once an association is made, it not only increases the probability that you will make the same association *but also decreases the probability you will see it any other way.* When you are wired to see condoms, you will see condoms! Even when you are looking at a tea bag, your prior experience will decrease the probability of seeing a tea bag and increase the probability of seeing a condom. When you are wired to see your partner as angry or mean, it decreases the probability you will see him any other way. He can be kind, supportive, loving, and you won't notice, but the first sign of any anger or meanness will immediately get your attention. *When you are wired to see negative, you will see negative!* This is a well-known phenomenon called "confirmation bias." And when you approach someone believing he or she will be negative, you will almost always get a negative response. That's why monocular vision is so destructive to relationships.

Assessing Your Monocular Vision

As we stated, your view of the world is greatly influenced by your past experiences. Most of the time this influence is not conscious, particularly when fear and shame are involved. Use the following exercises to get a reading on how your past might influence your perceptions today. Simply complete the sentences, writing down the first response that comes to mind.

Men are . . .

A man will always . . .

Men are good at . . .

My relationship with men throughout my life has been . . .

In a relationship, a man will . . .

You can always trust a man to . . .

Women are . . .

A woman will always . . .

Women are good at . . .

My relationship with women throughout my life has been . . .

In a relationship, a woman will . . .

You can always trust a woman to . . .

Sometimes completing these sentences gives you insight into your unconscious views of men and women. One woman in Pat's workshop remarked, "I knew these thoughts were somewhere back in my history. I just didn't realize how close to the surface they were—this exercise explains several of my past relationships." The answers she had written about men all had negative connotations, even though the sentence stems are neutral.

It is important to note that **negative perceptions from your past can be a prime source of fear and shame in the present.** Diana's fear came not from any of Brandon's actions but from her history with men. This fact is very relevant for those of us who have a history replete with fear and shame.

The Fire Hose Effect

There is another way to form a rut in a dirt pile that does not require repetition—take a fire hose to it! A powerful blast of water will make a rut, just as deep or deeper than years of normal rainfall. Trauma, which is any real or perceived threat, acts like water from fire hose. Traumatic events can include verbal, physical, or sexual abuse; public humiliation; job loss; financial failure; betrayal; rejection; neglect; violence; war; poverty—the list is long. Events that threaten physical, relational, or emotional safety leave a lasting impression. Someone who has experienced such traumatic events will have a hair-trigger response to fear- or shame-provoking events,* and there is only so much a partner can do to alleviate this pain. Certainly, avoiding any intentional acts that include triggering the hypersensitivity is the first way to help. Another way is by developing compassion about the discomfort and angst that come with these extreme emotional responses. And a third way to help is to practice the rituals of connection set forth in this book. The most effective strategies, however, must come from the individual with the reactive response of fear or shame. If the problem has advanced to the point where either of you feels that you have to walk on eggshells, we strongly suggest that you read Steven's book *You Don't Have to Take It Anymore.*

Twenty-Twenty Binocular Vision

With monocular vision you will be inclined to see what you have already seen, hear what you have already heard, and feel what you have already felt. In contrast, binocular vision takes in *new* information, which makes it possible for you to see your partner more or less objectively, integrating his or her positive and negative characteristics. But more than that, binocular vision includes *seeing your own behavior objectively*—and gives you a taste of what it is like living with you. Developing binocular vision takes a great deal of maturity because it requires getting out of the mental ruts we've formed and seeing the world through your partner's eyes as well as your own. Use the following exercise to see how close you are to twenty-twenty binocular vision.

*If you scored 20 or higher on the FID (fear, isolation, deprivation) index or the SIF (shame, inadequacy, failure) index, then it stands to reason you might have a hair-trigger reaction to fear- or shame-provoking events and deserve to move on from this vulnerable position by accepting the many resources available to you.

List three negative characteristics that you think describe your partner (for example, being angry, distant, selfish, preoccupied, nagging, unreasonable).

1. _____
2. _____
3. _____

Now list three positive characteristics you would like to see *more* of in your partner (for example, being affectionate, generous, helpful, or sexually excited).

1. _____
2. _____
3. _____

Look again at the negative characteristics you listed and describe how each one might also apply to you. For example, if you listed "angry" as number 1, then you might answer, "*My* anger shows up in the negative thoughts and judgments I have about my partner" or "*My* anger shows up with the kids." If you listed "distant," your answer might be, "I am distant in the bedroom when I avoid sex" or "I am distant when I withhold information from my partner."

Were you surprised at how easy it is to find your partner's faults in yourself? Binocular vision includes new information about your behavior as well as your partner's. If you found yourself squirming as you thought this through, you are well on your way to developing binocular vision. If you didn't squirm, you might need to engage the help of your partner to get a better reading on your own behavior.

How Do You Make It Hard for Your Partner to Give You What You Want?

The next step is even more difficult but well worth the effort. Go back and look at your list of positive characteristics you'd like to see more of in your partner. For each positive behavior, ask yourself **how you make it difficult** for your partner to be this way. For example, if you wrote that you would like your partner to be "more interested in sex" or "to be closer to me," your response might look something like this: "I make it difficult for my partner to *be more interested in sex* by *constantly complaining and ignoring her needs for intimacy*," or "I make it difficult for my partner to *be close to me* by *staying busy and never having a quiet moment.*" Again, you are looking for the squirm. The more insight and squirminess you have about your own behavior, the better your binocular vision.

How Could You Make It *Easier*?

This section is no walk in the park either. However, it is the logical next step for anyone truly interested in finding love beyond words. Look again at the positive characteristics you would like your partner to increase. For each item think about **how you could make it easier** for your partner. For example, if you wrote down that you would like your partner to be "more interested in sex" or "more fun," your response might look something like this: "To make her more interested in sex, *I could be more affectionate in nonsexual ways.*" "To make him have more fun, *I could join in the activities I know he enjoys.*"

Now you do it.

To make my partner more . . .

I could . . .

If you thought you could make your partner more lovable by changing your behavior, would you do it? Choose one of the behaviors you just wrote about and begin practicing. Change your own behavior but don't be surprised when your partner's behavior begins to change, too.

More Rewiring

Relationship dynamics shape the neurocircuitry of the brain just as much as individual experiences. If the condom/tea bag experience were repeated a few times—and fortunately for Brandon and Diana, it was not—Diana would have begun to associate her discomfort or pain, whatever the source, with something Brandon had done: *If I feel bad, you must be doing something wrong.* Brandon would have begun to associate her pain and discomfort with an inevitable accusation: *If she hurts, I'm in trouble.* He would then become defensive instead of compassionate when she was uncomfortable or in pain. **The natural compassion that couples have for each other gives way to a defensive resentment as they begin to expect the other to let them down or hurt them in some way.** They get trapped in a rigid, monocular vision that makes the beloved seem like an opponent rather than a partner.

Chances are, if you bought this book, you've become somewhat stuck in monocular vision.* But we're pleased to tell you that you are not *trapped* in it. You can change the way your brain is wired and begin to see life through a more enriching lens that includes your experiences as well as your partner's. Here are a few examples.

- ♥ *Understand the signals of anxiety, fear, and shame.* This will help enormously. If Diana had understood and "owned" her anxiety about the condom, she would have considered approaching Brandon

*Remember, this doesn't mean you are looking with one eye; it means you are not seeing your partner's perspective.

MONOCULAR VISION

My feelings don't matter to him.
↓
He doesn't love me.
↓
He's not going to get away with it!

in this way: "I'm just so sensitive that things like this send my anxiety through the roof and I overreact." Then Brandon could have soothed her anxiety rather than defending himself against the anger it triggered.

▾ *Associate your perspective with his.* Diana knew what it was like for her when she found what she thought was a condom, and her distress made her impugn her husband's character. But what was it like for *him*? Even if it had been a condom he'd overlooked, would that have meant that he didn't love her or didn't care about her feelings? How hurtful was it for him that she even *thought* the worst about him?

▾ *Associate the benefit of the doubt with discomfort and pain.* When you feel pain, practice thinking, "There's probably a good explanation— we'll work it out." So many heartaches could be prevented if couples gave each other the benefit of the doubt or simply paused to get more information. When you have a strong reaction to an everyday event your first response should be: "Hold on, let me listen and hear the other side."

▾ *Associate a positive image of your partner and relationship with your distress and pain.* The key to this technique is deciding what kind of image of your partner you want to nurture. Do you want to see him as a liar, a philanderer, or an insensitive lout or as a well-meaning man who has your best interests at heart but who occasionally makes mistakes? This is more than a variation on innocent until proven guilty; it forces you to add the perspective of your partner to your own, which is what binocular vision is all about. If you make this association repeatedly, it will forge new connections in your brain that will have profound effects on the state of your relationship.

SEEING YOUR PARTNER'S PERSPECTIVE ALONGSIDE YOUR OWN

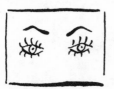

Diana's Perspective

My feelings don't matter to him.
↓
He doesn't love me.
↓
He's not going to get away with it!

Brandon's Perspective

I didn't notice it (if it had been a condom).
↓
I feel like a failure when she's unhappy.
↓
I can't make her happy.

Of course, much of the time you will not know what your partner's perspective is and therefore will not know what to associate with your distressed feelings. In that case, the reflex to develop is: Until you can find out your partner's perspective, yours is temporarily *incomplete,* which means you do not have enough data to come to a conclusion.

Never trust half the picture!

Binocular vision is about holding on to self-value *and* our value of loved ones in the face of disappointment. The ability to do the latter with any consistency depends on our ability to do the former. The most important thing we have to do when we feel devalued is to raise self-value, not indulge the re-

RECOGNIZING THAT YOUR VISION IS INCOMPLETE

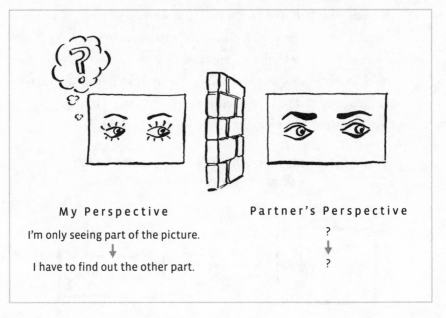

My Perspective

I'm only seeing part of the picture.
↓
I have to find out the other part.

Partner's Perspective

?
↓
?

venge motive of anger. Punishment of loved ones might make us feel tem-porarily more powerful but *not* more valuable. For example, the anger Diana felt when she mistook the tea bag for a condom came not from Brandon's action but from the meaning she gave to it. To her it meant that he didn't love her and that she was not worth his consideration. She made it about *her value* and not about his forgetfulness. Her anger was to punish him for low-ering her self-value. She made an enemy of the beloved.

Diana must understand that her value as a person is much too important to be diminished by what she found in the drawer, no matter what it was. She needs an internal mechanism of raising her self-value when it drops precipitously, such as thinking of the most important things about her as a person, feeling the love she has for the important people in her life, feeling her spiritual connection, imagining something she thinks is beautiful in na-ture, her favorite art or music, sense of friendship and community, and com-passionate things she has done. When she can do that, her negotiations with her husband will be about a behavior request, not her value as a per-son, and the emotional intensity will vanish. When we can hold on to self-

THE BINOCULAR VIEW

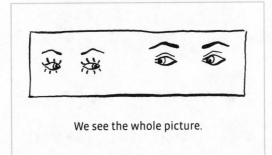

We see the whole picture.

value in the face of disappointment, we see ourselves and our loved ones in a much more positive light that naturally rewires our brain circuits for binocular vision.

The Single Most Important Thing to Do

Developing the ability to experience the world through your partner's eyes, while holding on to your own perspective, may be the single most important skill in intimate relationships. At the very least, it will give you an intuitive sense of how to improve your relationship without talking about it. In the next chapter, you'll see how binocular vision offers your best chance of having a great sex life, too.

the natural language
of binocular vision

When Sex Talks, Who Needs Words?

hen the relationship is on the rocks, the rocks are in the bed. No relationship issue has the ability to stir fear and shame like sex. And no relationship issue can benefit more from binocular vision than sex. While it's inaccurate to say that sex is the problem in all unhappy relationships, sex is a common casualty of unhappy relationships. Sex always makes the top-four list of subjects that couples fight about. The reason for this is simple: Sex is a powerful source of pleasure *and* a powerful source of pain. It can easily evoke fear in women and inadequacy in men, which makes it difficult to see each other's point of view or be rational about the subject.

Neither Kirsten nor Paul was in a rational place when they came to the couples' workshop. They had signed up mainly because they were tired of the incessant fighting and because their family therapist had recommended it. They had gone to therapy with their seven-year-old son, Jason, who was having problems in school, and during their second session the family counselor suggested they attend the couples' workshop to improve their relationship. (This made perfect sense, given the fact that research shows most acting-out behavior in children is correlated with unhappiness between the two parents.)

Kirsten and Paul had begun their relationship full of hope and passion, but by the second year they had fallen into a pattern of disconnection that began building a wall of resentment. After Jason was born, Kirsten's libido seemed to change. At first she thought it was due to the demands of the baby and sleep deprivation. Paul pitched in to help more, getting up nights with Jason to let Kirsten sleep. This helped her exhaustion but not her libido. She still didn't feel like having sex. They began leaving Jason with Paul's parents once a week so they could go out, but this didn't seem to make much difference either. The longer they went without sex, the more sullen and angry Paul became.

As their sexual frequency went down, the wall of resentment went up.

Paul became angrier, and Kirsten responded with anxiety and criticism. Occasionally she tried using affection to feel closer to him, but even that turned into an argument about sex. Now and then he tried being romantic, but she was too full of resentment to see it as anything but a ploy to get her in bed. The situation deteriorated, and in a few short years their sexual frequency went from having sex a couple times a week before Jason's birth to having sex just a few times a year by year five. When they came to the workshop they hadn't had sex for eight months, despite the fact that they each said their preference was to get back to a once-a-week schedule.

Paul was entrenched in his withdrawal and anger. He had consented to attend the workshop simply because he was too tired to argue. Kirsten hoped that the workshop would help Paul see how he was hurting her with his anger and making it impossible to feel sexual toward him. Her pain was so deep she couldn't see how she was contributing to their disconnection. But toward the end of the morning session, Kirsten began to see her role in their distance and disconnection. She realized that unknowingly she had taken a stance that could do nothing but build anger and resentment in Paul. Through one of the exercises, she began to see that, though she had never said these words, her actions had clearly said to Paul, *I expect you to be monogamous—but don't expect me to meet your sexual needs.* When the reality of her behavior hit her, fear and embarrassment flooded through her body. She felt the impact of her unrealistic position and the threat it posed to her relationship.

Kirsten was accurate in perceiving her stance as dangerous. You can *destroy* your relationship without talking just as you can *improve* your relationship without talking. Ignoring the importance of sex in a relationship is a very effective way to build resentment and destroy love. Don't get us wrong, if neither partner in the relationship is interested in sex or wants sex—no problem. But if one person wants sex, and he or she doesn't have sex—then the *relationship* has a problem. Kirsten could make the case that it didn't bother her much to go without sex, but because Paul desired sex, their infrequency of sexual contact put a strain on the relationship and the wall of resentment was a natural by-product.

What Happened?

Kirsten and Paul didn't set out to destroy their relationship. On the contrary, they fell in love and went through the throes of infatuation like many other couples. Early on, their sex life had been great. Kirsten watned sex as much as Paul, and she would initiate it often and respond readily to his sexual overtures. Because her sex drive was high during this time, Kirsten believed it would always be this way. What she didn't realize was that Nature gives your libido a boost in the early stage of love, but once this stage passes, you go back to your original sexual set point. In retrospect Kirsten could see that, other than during the romantic stage of a relationship, her libido had never been high. A saliva test for hormones showed that her testosterone level was low, explaining why she didn't feel the desire or urge to engage in sex very often. Paul, on the other hand, tested high in testosterone, so it was no surprise that his sex drive was high now and had always been high.

Moderate or high-desire persons* such as Paul walk around with sexual

*High desire refers to hormone levels, that is, high testosterone in men, high testosterone and estrogen in women. For more information about sexual desire, refer to *Hot Monogamy*, by Pat Love and Jo Robinson.

desire simmering right beneath the surface, ready at the least stimulation to be aroused. The high-desire person, male or female, doesn't have to work at getting aroused; it happens with normal stimulation. Once stimulated, the high-desire person moves step by step in a predictable, linear fashion to orgasm. The sexual-response cycle of a high- or moderate-testosterone person is shown in Figure 1.

What isn't obvious in Figure 1 is how uncomfortable the high-desire person becomes when he or she goes for a long period without sex. The low-desire person has trouble understanding how physically, emotionally, and psychologically uncomfortable it is to go without sexual relief, because this is not his or her experience. You can see why Paul became increasingly resentful when Kirsten ignored his sexual needs. It made no sense to him for her to withhold sex. In fact, it seemed cruel.

Kirsten's low level of testosterone explained why she knew in her heart that she wanted to be sexual with Paul, but rarely *felt* like doing it. Her heart would make a promise that her body wouldn't keep. Take a look at Figure 2, which depicts the sexual-response cycle of the low-desire person, and pay attention to your first impression.

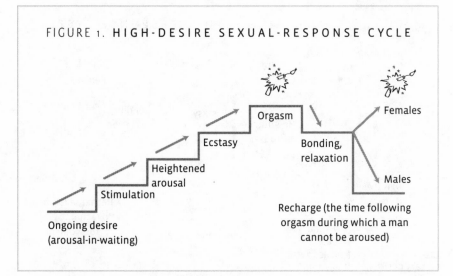

FIGURE 1. HIGH-DESIRE SEXUAL-RESPONSE CYCLE

Orgasm

Ecstasy

Heightened arousal

Stimulation

Ongoing desire (arousal-in-waiting)

Bonding, relaxation

Females

Males

Recharge (the time following orgasm during which a man cannot be aroused)

As you look at Figure 2, do you get a sense of the chaotic, inexplicable nature of this cycle? The low-desire person doesn't walk around with combustible sexual desire lying just beneath the surface. Even when stimulated, he or she may not feel the desire to have sex. In fact, *most low-desire individuals do not feel the desire to have sex until they are highly aroused!* You only want it when you are already doing it. In other words, you've got to do it to want it. This goes against everything we've been taught about sex. Understanding the nature of this low-desire set point is made even more difficult because during the infatuation stage of a relationship, the low-desire person looks, acts, and feels like a high-desire person. And it is human nature to think that it will always be this way. What isn't evident in Figure 2 is how hard the low-desire person has to work to create sexual desire. He or she has to focus, concentrate, motivate, wake up a sleeping body, and trust that desire will come somewhere down the line.

Once Kirsten began to understand her sexual-response cycle better, many aspects of her relationship with Paul began to make sense. She understood why every time they had sex she would say to herself: "This is wonderful. I'm going to remember to do it more often!" She also understood

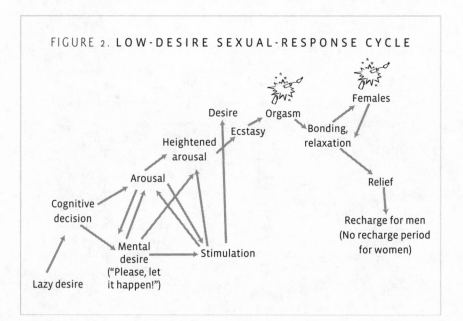

FIGURE 2. LOW-DESIRE SEXUAL-RESPONSE CYCLE

that she didn't keep this promise to herself because she unconsciously expected to feel desire before she was aroused. Plus, going without sex was not physically uncomfortable for her. It somehow went against her romantic heart to believe that one would have to work at getting aroused with someone you love.

Although the insight and understanding related to sexual desire was interesting and helpful, it did not change or improve the relationship much. The transformation did not come until Kirsten realized how self-absorbed she had been about their sexual relationship. Once she understood the fear-shame dynamic, it hit her that when she withheld sex, she was thinking only of what *she* felt like doing—or not doing. She was not thinking of Paul's needs and the shame he felt when she withheld the physical love she used to give so readily. Just as important, she was ignoring *the needs of the relationship*. She had said to herself time and time again, "Why should I do anything I don't want to do?" and felt perfectly justified in her position. She somehow felt that it was Paul's fault that she didn't feel aroused like she used to feel. After all, he turned her on in the beginning of the relationship, why couldn't he do it now? In the end, getting information, taking responsibility, and experiencing the embarrassment and remorse of her actions changed her and the relationship permanently. Once she connected the feeling of remorse to withholding sex, she could no longer ignore Paul's needs or the needs of the relationship.

Why the Hype About Sex?

It's funny how sex factors into the way people describe the state of their relationships. Studies show that, when things are going well, sex contributes only 15 percent to the overall satisfaction of a relationship. But if things aren't going well, it contributes 85 percent to the dissatisfaction. This is partly because a good sex life augments other areas of satisfaction so that it becomes one of many good things happening in the relationship. But it is also due to the power of sex to stir the old fear-shame dynamic. Once activated, the fear-shame whirlwind diminishes all other areas of intimacy and connection so that sex, as a *symbol* of intimacy and connection, seems to be a major factor in the disappointment people feel about their relationships.

There's another reason to stress the importance of sex—it's good for your physical and mental health, as long as it's fully consensual. Pat still has to laugh at this statement. When she began the research for her book *Hot Monogamy,* she secretly hoped to find that mature, highly evolved, intelligent beings didn't want or need sex, that it was only the lower animals, way down the food chain, who made sex a priority. You can probably guess that she hoped that because her own sexual desire was very low. Alas, this is not what she found. She found that, indeed, sex has many advantages to both people involved. Here are just a few.

Twenty Reasons to Have Sex When You Don't Feel Like It

1. Because you said so. Even though you may not have promised to "love, honor, and have sex once a week" when you made a commitment to your relationship, it was understood that sex would be part of the bargain. Imagine how the marriage rates would go down if people said, "I'll marry you, but don't expect sex." If you polled one thousand people on the street and asked them, "Is it reasonable to expect to have sex when you are married?" the overwhelming majority would say yes. If you expect a monogamous commitment from your partner, then it stands to reason that you will be a cooperative sex partner.

2. Sex helps you forget. Oxytocin, which triggers orgasm, has an amnesic effect that lasts up to five hours. So for a period of time you forget that he maxed out your Visa card or she was an hour late getting home from work. Women get an additional benefit. During orgasm the parts of the brain that govern fear, anxiety, and stress are switched off. (Faking orgasm gives no such benefit.)

3. Sex rewires you for pleasure. Every time you share a positive experience with your partner, your brain comes to associate him or her with pleasure. You can transform any relationship simply by increasing the number of enjoyable times you share together.

4. Sex puts the "P" back in partnership. Passion is what separates your relationship with your intimate partner from those with girlfriends and buddies. Yes, you two are best friends and confidants, but without sex you will not have passion.

The following are from a 1997 study in the *British Medical Journal*.

5. Heightened sense of smell. After sex, production of prolactin surges, causing stem cells in the brain to develop new neurons in the brain's smell center (olfactory bulb).

6. Weight loss. Rambunctious sex burns a minimum of two hundred calories, about the same as running fifteen minutes on a treadmill. British researchers determined that the equivalent of six Big Macs can be worked off by having sex three times a week for a year.

7. Reduced depression. Prostaglandin, a hormone found in semen, modulates female hormones. Orgasm releases endorphins, producing a sense of well-being and euphoria.

8. Pain relief. During sex, levels of oxytocin surge to five times their normal level, releasing endorphins that alleviate pain. Sex also prompts production of estrogen, which reduces the pain of PMS.

9. Healthier heart. Women who have more sex have higher levels of estrogen, which protects against heart disease.

10. Cure for the common cold. Once-a-week sex produces 30 percent higher levels of immunoglobulin A, which boosts the immune system.

11. Better bladder control. Sex strengthens the pelvic muscles that control the flow of urine.

12. Peppy prostate. Some urologists believe they see a relationship between infrequency of ejaculation in men and cancer of the prostate. In this case solo sex works just as well, but why miss out on all the other benefits?

13. Shiny hair, glowing skin. For women, extra estrogen from orgasm makes hair shine. Sweat produced during sex cleanses the pores and makes skin glow. Serotonin produces the afterglow of sex.

14. Calming effect. Sex is ten times more effective than Valium, with no side effects.

15. Relief for a stuffy nose. Really. Sex is a natural antihistamine. It can even help combat hay fever and asthma.

16. Firmer tummy and butt. Regular sex can firm your tummy and butt, plus improve posture.

17. Boosts your immune system. Endorphins stimulate immune-system cells that fight disease.

18. Forever young. Sex actually slows the aging process. It lowers cortisol levels in the bloodstream, which reduces stress and slows the aging process.

19. Protection against Alzheimer's and osteoporosis. Women who have more sex have higher levels of estrogen, which protects against Alzheimer's and osteoporosis.

20. Euphoria. Who wouldn't want more? The best way to get a natural high is sex!

Changing Horses in Midstream

In most couples both parties will tell you that they desire to have a more active, loving sexual relationship. They agree on the ultimate goal—how to get there is the problem. A rational approach says, "Well, if you both want the same thing, why don't you just do it?" Easier said than done. Because sex has a powerful effect on the fear-shame dynamic, the rational part of your brain is not always in charge (otherwise we'd have a lot fewer sex-related problems in our culture). Here are just a few examples of what goes on.

When a woman refuses sex, a man typically thinks, *I'm not important* or *I'm inadequate as a lover.* Shame prompts him to be angry or shut down. If a woman wants sex and the man refuses, he gets a double dose of inadequacy: *I'm a failure as a partner and as a man.* When he refuses her, she often thinks, *I'm not attractive* or *He doesn't love me,* which activates her fears and evokes a blame/complain response. When a woman refuses sex it's often because she just doesn't feel like having sex, yet she consciously or unconsciously blames him for her lack of response. Her refusal can also trigger her fear of isolation and or harm and motivate her to seek comfort through other means, such as work, friends, children, busyness, eating, or spending.

The more fear-shame responses you have experienced pertaining to your sex life, the stronger your resistance will be to change. The good news is: You can do it anyway. The discomfort of resistance lasts only a few seconds unless you dwell on it. Plus, the greater the resistance, the greater the sense of empowerment you feel when you take charge. Here's a tip: **Feel the discomfort—and forge ahead.** Now here are three suggestions on how to proceed.

1. Just say yes. This means anytime one person wants sex, the answer is yes. The thought of this usually delights the high-desire person and scares the low-desire person. Both may initially have visions of never getting out of

bed. But hang on. You will both be surprised at how well this works. When sex is readily available, it becomes far less of an issue. The anxiety of deprivation is gone; the dread of making excuses is gone; the guilt of withholding is gone. Talk about a great way to improve your relationship without talking!

Kirsten and Paul took this approach. They were delighted to find that they weren't far off in their preferences. Initially he made a request for sex more often than Kirsten would have liked, but after two weeks, the frequency leveled out and when they checked in at the three-month period, they couldn't even pinpoint how many times they had sex per week or month. It had become a nonissue. They were basically having sex in rhythm with their life—and both were satisfied.

2. You say when, I say what. Sometimes sex is easier said than done—especially if you are equating sex with intercourse. A woman can lubricate herself and be physically receptive to sex, but it's not always that easy for a man. He has to get an erection, which may require a little more forethought and foreplay. So if the woman says when, he can say what, meaning what type of sex they have. He may choose to start off with oral sex to stimulate an erection. He may suggest that they start off by watching a sexy movie. The "what person" may also opt for a quickie, giving the "when person" an orgasm but saving his for later. It's probably not a good idea for the "what person" to suggest 68 (you do me and I owe you one).

3. Role reversal. Many times couples get polarized around sex negotiation. One says, "I want more sex," while the other says, "I want more intimacy." One needs connection to have sex; the other needs sex to have connection. Both are telling the truth. In the role-reversal option the high-desire person is in charge of the intimacy and the low-desire person is in charge of the sex. The person who wants more sex makes sure the other partner gets plenty of intimacy. The person who wants more intimacy makes sure the other partner gets plenty of sex. Each person gets the desired outcome; the roles are just reversed.

Role reversal requires maturity and understanding. The low-desire person should at least have some memory of wanting sex from the infatuation stage of the relationship; what may not be included in that memory, however, is how uncomfortable it is to go without sex. This is not the experience of the low-desire person, who feels just fine going without sex. The low-desire person will just have to take our word for it—or better yet, take his or her partner's word for it.

Here's what happens if you're a high-desire person and you go without sex. Your body tightens, you have trouble sleeping, you can't rest, sexual thoughts occupy your mind, and sex becomes far more important than it should be. Sexual tension is a lot like a migraine. It starts off with early warning signs like an aura or mild discomfort, which can lead to distorted thinking, irritability, and ultimately throbbing pain throughout your body. Imagine you have a migraine and your partner ignores your pain as you suffer day after day. No extensions of caring like "How are you feeling?" or "Honey, is there anything I can do to help?" Or, worse yet, imagine that your partner has the relief-giving potion but won't give it to you.

Here are some tips to get you on your way.

Tips for the high-desire person: Be responsible for your partner's need for intimacy. This means stuff like nonsexual touching, saying "I love you," smiling, making eye contact, whispering sweet nothings (again, no sex talk), asking "How was your day?" and then listening. Telling him or her one thing you liked about your day and one thing you didn't like about your day or simply sharing more of the responsibilities. Above all: When asked to connect to your partner before sex, do not question it or talk about it, do not argue, do not try to understand; accept his or her reality on faith—just do it. It can't hurt, and it might help!

Tips for the low-desire person: Be a responsible sex partner. Pay attention to your partner's need for sex as well as the relationship's need for sex. Avoid judging, criticizing, or making excuses. Resist the temptation to keep score—count how many times your partner tunes in to your intimacy needs.

Focus on what you are giving, not what you are getting. Take pleasure in pleasing your partner. Become an expert in your own sexual arousal; take care of yourself in a way that will enable you to enjoy sex and look forward to it.

The high-desire person has a steep learning curve, too, because he or she doesn't understand how much effort is required for the low-desire person to get aroused. It takes extreme concentration, plus the faith that you will ultimately get to arousal. Imagine this scenario: You had a long, hard day at work, drove forty-five minutes in traffic, got home, cooked dinner, did the dishes, helped with homework, cleaned the litter box, settled two sibling disputes, did three loads of laundry, and all you can think about is precious sleep—but when you open the bedroom door there is a fifty-foot tightrope between you and the bed. Not only that, your partner is already in bed and hot to trot. What is your response if your partner says, "Hurry up and get over here, I'm ready for sex"? Would you respond differently if your partner said, "There's my sweetheart. I'll come over and help you across the tightrope; you're so desirable"? Or what if you came home and your partner had greeted you with a hug and kiss, had dinner started, had already cleaned the litter box, and done two loads of laundry? How would that affect your response? When the low-desire person says, "I need to feel connected to have sex," another way to say this is "Give me something to work with. Jump-start my motivation."

Changing Needs

If you live long enough and/or stay with the same partner long enough, you will each need a different type of stimulation to keep sex fresh and exciting. Most couples who are dissatisfied with sex and/or intimacy are simply in need of a few changes in their repertoire, but initiating these changes can evoke fear in women and inadequacy in men. If a woman expresses interest in a new sexual practice a man might think, *I'm not good enough* or *What if I can't perform? Does this mean she's dissatisfied with me? I don't know if I can live up to her expectations. Have I not been pleasing her? Where did she come up with an idea like this? How long has she been unhappy? Is there someone else?* If a man expresses interest in a new sexual practice a woman might think, *Will he get angry if I say no? Will he leave me if I don't satisfy him? Will he pull away from me if I don't give him what he wants? Do I have to do everything he wants to keep him? If I say yes, what will he require of me next?*

Ironically, the very changes that are needed to provide the excitement that will help deepen the connection provoke anxiety because they threaten the *stability* of the connection. Couples establish routines for a reason. Constancy, like commitment, is comforting. But the more comfortable you get, the less exciting your sex life becomes—unless you simply take steps to change it.

Lack of excitement may not be the sole reason one or both of you need to make changes in your sex life. The fact is, over time men and women both need to change foreplay and sex play to achieve a satisfactory level of arousal. For example, in the early years of a woman's life the simple act of the penis entering the vagina sends a wave of pleasure through her body comparable to orgasm. Over time, she requires not only penetration but also clitoral stimulation to be highly aroused. This is why couples who may not start out practicing oral sex or manual stimulation often change their foreplay practices to include these types of stimulation. Men in the early years are easily aroused by visual stimulation. Simply watching his partner undress can arouse a high-desire man. As he ages, visual stimulation still does the trick, but a more provocative form—for example, watching his partner stimulate herself or stimulate him—may be required.

Since changing sexual needs is such an important aspect of ongoing relationship improvement, perhaps a short exercise might be helpful. Complete the following sentences by yourself.

1. In terms of sex and intimacy, what I would like from my partner is . . . (examples: to initiate sex more, to be willing to try new things, to help more around the house, to be more affectionate).

2. One way I have made it difficult for him or her to give this to me is . . . (examples: I have not let him or her know how important this is to me, I criticize the help he or she does give me, I withhold affection).

3. One way I could make it easier for him or her to give this to me is to . . . (examples: let him or her know how important this is to me by writing a love letter, ask for help around specific household tasks that are easily accomplished and then show appreciation when they are done, be affectionate in the ways I know he/she loves).

Once you complete the exercise, do not talk about it and do not share your answers. Instead, go right to the heart of the matter:

- Quit doing number 2. Start doing number 3!
- Show appreciation. Watch for any form of number 1, and when you see it, acknowledge it in a loving manner.

Happy couples have figured out that sex is a great way to improve the relationship without talking. In this day of preventive health care and lifestyle enhancement, there is no sexual problem that doesn't have a solution. Any man can get an erection; any woman can achieve sexual satisfaction—and if you work as a team, the sky's the limit. Teamwork requires binocular vision—a way of looking at sex from your partner's perspective as well as your own.

In the next chapter you'll see how binocular vision enables you to learn the most healing skill in relationships, one that is absolutely necessary to gain a love beyond words.

eleven

the only connection skill you need

Stepping into the Puddle

Once you've recognized what your deepest values are and are committed to seeing your partner's perspective as equal to your own, you're ready to learn the ultimate connection skill. If there were such a thing as a cure-all for disconnection, it would be *conscious* emotional attunement, which is literally tuning in to the emotional state of another. We call it "stepping into the puddle." In Chapter 4 we talked about the negative power of *un*conscious emotional attunement and how you probably have developed defenses against it when the emotions of your partner are negative. Maybe, if you're a woman, you've tried to comfort the man in your life in the way you would comfort a woman and got rejected: "You seem upset about your job, let's talk about it." Or worse, you might have been so self-focused that you refused to acknowledge his dread of shame or that he had a "right" to feel the way he did. Or perhaps you fretted, "If he loses his job, what will we do?" If you're a man, you may have tried to tell your partner what she should do to feel better, only to have her get upset with you. Or worse, you told her something like "You brought it on yourself—you should have seen it coming."

Healthy emotional attunement requires you to manage your own fear, dread, insensitivity, and the negative judgments that go with them. If you're a woman, it requires that you tune in to your man's dread of shame. If you do this, something magical will happen. As you focus on his dread of shame rather your own resentment, you will lower your own fear and increase the likelihood of connection. Likewise, men must tune in to their partner's anxiety. Guys, if you focus on her fear rather than your urge to withdraw, you will lower your discomfort and increase the likelihood of connection.

It's a Puddle, Not an Ocean

Some people worry that if they actually tuned in and felt their partners' discomfort, they would fall into an ocean of pain from which they would never emerge. We don't want to seem sarcastic, but take moment to think about how crazy that is. Emotional attunement is a *survival* mechanism. There would be no evolutionary advantage or God-given purpose in drowning us in oceans of negativity. That wouldn't help anyone survive. **Emotional attunement is designed to connect you for your mutual benefit.**

To get the point of stepping into the puddle, you have to think only about the early part of your relationship before resentment took over. When your partner felt irritated, angry, depressed, anxious, worried, or tense, you did not *ignore* those feelings or take them personally, nor did they suck you into the depths of emotional despair or turmoil. You let him or her know that you cared, and, chances are, you got the same caring from your partner when you were down or upset. Your interest in each other's well-being is what made you both feel better. But chances are, our women readers did not express that interest with something like "Oh, honey, what's wrong?" or "Tell me how you feel" or "We need to talk." The response then would have been the same as now: "Nothing's wrong, I'm fine" or "I'm just tired." He might have done it more politely then than he would now, but he still would have blown you off had you been that direct. And, guys, you didn't express your interest or caring about her feelings by changing the subject or pretending you didn't notice or by grumbling, "It's always something with her."

You most likely expressed your interest in the well-being of your partner indirectly—without talking about your relationship—by "stepping into the puddle." You could have done this in any number of ways: touched hands, rubbed shoulders, commiserated, supported, believed in each other, hugged, put flowers on the table, played music the other liked, *and*—this is the most important part—allowed yourself to feel whatever he or she was feeling. When you did that, you did not sink into a bottomless ocean of despair; you most likely found that the negativity was just a puddle, and you were able to step out of it *together*. Here's an example.

Brad felt too exhausted to let Krissy know that he'd come home from work. When she found him in the den, spread-eagled on the sofa, she felt a bit offended that he hadn't sought her out to say hello. Her instinct was to tell him how important it was to "communicate appropriately," to "have common courtesy," and so on. Luckily, she knew about "stepping into the puddle" and saw a chance to put it into practice. She sat down beside her tired husband, with her shoulders barely touching his. She adjusted her breathing to his. She *felt* his exhaustion. After about three minutes of silence, she started rubbing his back, which he let her do for a while, before, much to her surprise, he started rubbing hers.

"I really needed that," he said. "How was your day?"

That's right; *he* asked *her* how her day was. That's the kind of thing that happens when you're connected.

The bottom line is: **Be there with your partner's feelings. Don't ignore them, try to "fix it," or try to talk about it or *drag* him or her out of it.** Many times, stepping into the puddle with the man in your life involves simply noticing his discomfort and honoring his space with silence and support. And many times, it is just sympathetic eye contact with the woman in your life to let her know that you "get" her. Whatever form it takes in your relationship, if you *model* stepping into the puddle for your partner, you will most likely get the same in return.

Why You *Have* to Step into the Puddle

It's understandable that you might be reluctant to step into the puddle with your partner; after all, no one wants to sit with negative emotions even for a short time. But there are three compelling reasons why you *have* to do it. The first is that it forges a closer connection—you do far more to build intimacy and trust by helping each other with negative emotions than by sharing only positive ones. Second, failing to connect with your sad or distressed partner actually makes it harder for him or her to transform negative emotions than if you weren't there at all. You can hardly shift to the positive while reacting to someone you love ignoring you, rejecting you, or trying to control you by implying that you're incompetent. This is an important point about parenting, too. You're not going to help your sons and daughters by telling them that they *shouldn't* feel the way they do. You'll help them by being in the emotion with them for a few moments while they work their own way out of it.

The third reason that stepping into the puddle is necessary in intimate relationships is that you promised to do it! (You made an implicit promise to each other that you would always *care* when the other feels bad.) You wouldn't have formed a bond in the first place unless you both believed that the other would care when you felt bad. When you were forging your emotional bonds, you did not say, "I'll only care about you when it's convenient for me and when I feel like it." You promised then—through your caring behavior—to care *whenever* necessary. So when one of you fails to do it now, the other feels betrayed.

Do not try to step into the puddle to further your own agenda. You must not tune in to your partner's emotional state just so he or she will listen to what you have to say—if you even try that, it will seem artificial. You must step fully into the puddle and forget about your own agenda, until you both step fully out of it. It will take a lot of concentration in the beginning, but it gets easier as you get used to it. You'll love the results.

Stepping into the Puddle with Him

When you step into the puddle with a man, be sure that you are not trying to do it in the same way you would with your girlfriends. "Oh, honey, what's wrong, let's talk!" will work well with a female friend; she'll feel better just because you're trying to connect with her. But a man will often need connection plus *action* to feel better. For example, Sherry took her teenage grandson, Derek, on vacation to Europe. In their hotel room one night after dinner, she overheard him talking to his parents about some fun activity the family was doing back home. She could tell when he hung up that he felt homesick and left out.

"Oh, Derek, that must be disappointing, missing out on that. I know you were looking forward to it. You must really feel bad."

"Grandma," he groaned, "you're making it worse!" Sherry's gut reaction was to feel rejected and shut out by her grandson's cold reaction to her sincere attempts to comfort him. Then she realized that she was treating him as if he were a little girl, for whom talking about it would have been a big help. She hugged her grandson briefly and asked if he wanted to play cards. Within a few minutes of playing cards, he felt much better.

In general the formula for stepping into the puddle with a male is:

- Make some physical gesture that you're there with him.
- Be available to do something that he's good at. This replaces his sense of failure with a sense of competence and mastery.

Stepping into the Puddle with Her

Over 70 percent of divorce is initiated by women who think their husbands don't care about how they feel. That's really sad because we have met very few men who, unless they were angry at that moment, did not care a great deal about how their wives felt. In fact, it was the unhappiness of their wives that made them feel like failures and withdraw or get angry in the first place. We're convinced that most men *want* to show that they care; they just need a skill to help them do it in a way that doesn't make them feel like women. The skill is "stepping into the puddle," where the "puddle" is whatever negative feelings she is experiencing at that moment. We don't mean superficial negative feelings that will pass on their own in a few minutes. We mean more of a *funky mood;* when she feels nervous, stressed, upset, or depressed—she might call it icky. Your instinctive protectiveness might drive you to get her out of the puddle as soon as you can, by throwing her a life preserver or trying to drag her out of it—that is, fix the problem or tell her how to fix it. You have no doubt tried this many times in the past, only to meet her resentment, anger, or her accusation that you just "don't get it." Most men then begin to withdraw or try to ignore the puddle, which exaggerates their partners' fear of isolation. The fatal blow to most marriages occurs when a woman goes through an extended puddle, like an illness, emotional disorder, or death in the family, and her man withdraws from her to keep from being "dragged down by her negativity," as many of our male clients have put it. Once she comes out of the puddle, she feels that her man won't be there for her when she really needs him. She feels alone and isolated, often like a single parent. As a result, she ends the relationship.

It's especially important to step into the puddle with her during small funks. This will not only convince her that you can do it with big issues but will serve to *prevent* most of the big issues. Here's an example. Becky got a sinking feeling whenever she had to talk to her ex-husband about their kids. He could still push all her buttons five years after their divorce. Kenny, her current husband, would get so angry at her ex for upsetting her that she had grown hesitant to let him know when she was distraught. If he found out, all he would do was tell her how she *should* respond to her ex's badgering and negative attitude. "You should tell him that you're taking him to court and not put up with his crap," Kenny would say, which overwhelmed Becky with more anxiety. Eventually he'd get mad at her for not leaping to follow his instructions, and they would likely not speak to each other for the rest of the night. Instead of supporting her in the stress of dealing with her ex, Kenny greatly added to it. But after working with us, Kenny took a new approach. Sensing the distress that Becky tried to hide from him, he put his arms around her and told her how much he admired her for putting up with her ex-husband's mind games for the sake of her children. Becky complained for a while about the outrageous things her ex-husband had said on the phone, like insisting that she change the plane tickets for the girls' return home, meaning that she would have to pay a penalty to the airline. She vented about how unreasonable and unfair he was. Instead of cursing out her ex-husband and telling her what she should think about him, like he had the urge to do, Kenny merely agreed with her appraisal. He felt her anxiety and frustration. He sensed her fear that her children might be harmed if conditions between their parents got any worse. He pointed out how lucky the girls were to have such a considerate mother. Becky felt better immediately. She called her ex and renegotiated the airline tickets, for which Kenny congratulated her. They had a pleasant evening, feeling closer than ever before.

The bottom line is: **Be there with her. Don't ignore it; don't "fix" it, tell her what to do, or try to *drag* her out of it.** If you're just there with her a short time, the two of you can usually step out of the puddle *together*.

Beyond Survival

In Part I, we discussed the *survival* advantage of emotional attunement, which gives it a natural bias toward negative stimulation. It's more important to survival to pay attention to anger and aggression than to hope or appreciation, because anger and aggression can signal a threat to your life. This negative bias explains why it is *easier* to remember the bad times than the good. Nevertheless, learning to tune in to the good times is worth the effort, because tuning in to your partner provides some of the most beautiful experiences in relationships. The following true story about Rosa and Kevin illustrates this truth in a touching way.

Camille and Rosa had been friends since high school. Together, they went through marriage, divorce, remarriage, raising kids, changing jobs—you name it. The year they turned fifty they even joined the Red Hat Society together. When Camille died, Rosa's world was turned upside down. Her husband, Kevin, came close to understanding the significance of the loss and stood by lovingly through day after day of her grief. Ten months after Camille's death, with Thanksgiving looming, the loss felt even greater, because Rosa and Camille had always made tamales together on this day. Every year they had repeated the tradition: football on television, tamales in the kitchen. Rosa struggled with the decision whether or not to make the tamales this year, and finally decided that she would. But when she woke on Thanksgiving morning, she didn't know how she could get through the day. Pulling on her bathrobe, she shuffled to the kitchen to begin making the tamales alone. But as soon as she entered the kitchen she realized she was not alone at all. There on the counter, where Kevin had carefully placed them, were all the ingredients for tamales: corn meal, eggs, chilies, corn husks—plus her red hat.

Kevin stepped into the puddle with Rosa and helped her out with his simple but beautiful gesture of attunement, love, and compassion.

Who Said Connection Would Always Be Easy?

Here's a complaint we get from some women in our workshops: "I wanted to talk to him about something that was important to me. He rolled his eyes and sat down at the kitchen table, like I was telling him he had to repaint all the white stripes on the highway. 'Are you going to listen to me or what?' I asked him. 'Do I have a choice?' he asked with disgust in his voice. 'Yes, you have a choice,' I said. And he immediately gets up and just walks out on me. How the hell am I supposed to feel connected to him then?'"

First of all, if she felt connected to him *before* she wanted to talk, it probably would have sounded less like he was being asked to repaint all the white stripes on Route 66. Remember, the fear-shame dynamic is a signal of disconnection. Before you can *talk*, you have to *connect*. This is so important that it's worth an experiment. For five minutes before you want to talk to your man about something, do not think of what you want to *say*. Instead, try to imagine feeling close to him. Think of times when you felt close in the past. Think of times you watched sunsets together, tended the children together, went to church or to the movies together, smelled flowers together, or made love. Think of how you would want to feel close to him if a meteor was on the way and the world were going to end in the next couple of hours. Think of when you believed in him and were proud of him.

After about five minutes of this, you are ready to talk to him. Start by touching him, *still* without thinking of what you want to say. Feel his importance to you and your value of him in the touch. Then softly engage him in nonaccusing, nonblaming talk.

Don't say, "I need you to pick up the towel in the bathroom."

Say something like "Honey, I really get turned on when I see that you've hung up your towel, because I know you did it just for me." If that sounds unrealistic, give it a try. Appreciation can be a potent aphrodisiac.

To have satisfying talks with your man, you have to remember that emotions are more physically uncomfortable for him due to the greater arousal level and blood flow to his muscles. Let him fidget or do something with his hands, or better yet, go for a nice walk and talk. This will be different from what you have with your girlfriends, but it will still feel good.

Remember also that if you say something like "I feel isolated, like I'm not getting my needs met, and you take me for granted, just want me for sex, etc.," all he hears is "The way you love isn't good enough," and he gets defensive, angry, or aggressive, or he shuts down. You have a much better chance of connecting (reducing your anxiety and soothing his shame) by activating his *protectiveness,* and you have the best chance of doing that by exposing your own shame. Try something like: "Sometimes I really feel like a failure. People don't respect me, and I'm not all I could be as a lover."

His likely response will be protective and reassuring. He'll try to connect with you. In other words, he'll connect to your shame, and then you can expose your anxiety.

Okay, so you've tried all the above, and he still huffs out of the room, saying, "Leave me alone!" Yes, even then you can still feel connected to him, despite feeling resentful and angry. You can still feel like he's important to you and that these negative feelings will pass. Always ask yourself what is more important to you, the towel on the floor (or whatever you're resentful about) or feeling connected? What is more likely to get the towel hung up, resentment and bitterness or feeling connected? Is the most important thing about you as a person getting the towel hung up, or caring for your family? Ask yourself, "How can I help him with his shame?"

- Believe in him; see his good points, as you did when you first fell in love.
- Help him be a good lover. Let him know how he pleases you and what especially pleases you.
- Help him make you happy. The angry, controlling, or shut-down male is trying to avoid feeling like a failure because he hasn't been able to make you happy. Tell him how unhappy you are, and you risk losing him. Focus on how he makes you happy, and he will do more of it.
- Accept that he, too, has the best interests of your children at heart even when you disagree with his parenting style and then negotiate respectfully about specific parenting issues.
- Let him know what he does to make you feel safe and secure.
- Let him know that you appreciate his work.

- ♥ Respect him.
- ♥ Receive his repair attempts. If your man was forced to apologize as a child—and most little boys are—apology will likely feel more like submission than reconciliation; he will have trouble starting repair with an apology in the way that your girlfriends can. He is more likely to try repair *behaviorally*, by trying to resume routine connection, doing something for you, doing something with you, touching, or kissing. See these small things as gestures of your importance to him. They may not be eloquent, but they are sincere expressions of love for you and a symbol of your importance to him.

Here's a complaint we get from some men at our workshops: "I do everything she wants. But every little negative feeling she has is somehow my fault. There's no pleasing her." How many men have you heard say something like that? Actually, it's not that hard to please her if you pay attention to her anxiety signals, which you *know* she is putting out—your own level of discomfort tells you.

- ♥ Respect her.
- ♥ Listen to her.
- ♥ Express confidence in her.
- ♥ Help her as much as you can.
- ♥ Touch her more, but try to make it eight affectionate, *nonsexual* touches for every one sexual touch.
- ♥ Respect her bonds with her family and friends.
- ♥ Apologize if you fail to do any of the above.
- ♥ Receive her repair attempts if she offends you.
- ♥ Above all, step into the puddle with her.

"Stepping into the puddle" will usually reconnect you at times when your partner is distressed or feeling down. The next chapter offers the easiest way to maintain connection every day, without talking about it.

if you want connection, forget "feelings," think *motivation*

the ability to step into the puddle with your partner will reestablish connection when he or she is feeling down or distressed. Fortunately, maintaining connection is much easier on a routine basis. The trick is that all feelings boil down to one of three modes: approach, avoid, or attack. The more you can stay in approach mode, the happier you will be and the more satisfying your relationship will become.

The most important part of your emotions is not how they make you *feel* but what they get you to *do*. The primary function of emotions is to prepare us for action. The root meaning of word *emotion* is not "to feel" but "to *move*." The ancient Greeks described how emotions "moved behavior." In modern times we say they *motivate* behavior. Emotions send biological action signals to our muscles and organs to prepare us to *do* something. The way we feel when we have an emotion is the body's way of getting our attention to make us act on it. For the most part, we become aware of negative feelings when we do *not* do what they prepare us to do—that's when they start to feel bad. The pain in your foot gets you to loosen the laces of your shoes. The pain in your heart tells you to be true to the *most important* things about you.

It is much easier, especially for a man, to identify and change motivations than to figure out feelings. (Remember, dialogues about "feelings" are not a man's native language.) You are both likely to get frustrated trying to talk about emotional subjects, in part because there are dozens of variations on feelings, influenced by things like metabolism, temperament, health, rest, hormones, hunger, exercise, and medications, as well as the weather, season, and time of day. As if that weren't complex enough, the many permutations of feelings become associated with thousands of different experiences over the course of a lifetime. For instance, you may have associated feeling shame with your mother's raised eyebrow, your father calling you a "pain in the ——," or a teacher who made you feel dumb. Any of these experiences—or anything remotely like them—can trigger confusing "feelings" under the "wrong" circumstances. In contrast, *motivation* is far easier for a man—or a woman—to figure out. There are only three basic motivations, and each remains consistently associated with its separate but very broad category of behaviors throughout life.

APPROACH

AVOID

ATTACK

Approach means going toward someone or something with positive energy. In approach mode you want to get more of something, experience more, discover more, learn more, or appreciate more. You're in approach as you watch a sunset, try to solve a problem, or get interested in something. (When we say someone is approachable, we mean they are easily engaged in conversation, open to new information and ideas, friendly, interested, and amenable.) Ask yourself, "How do I feel when my partner approaches me with interest and a desire to learn or care about me?" Then ask yourself, "Do I want my partner to feel *that* way or do I want him or her to get defensive?"

Avoid means giving no energy at all. In avoid mode you want to get away from something or get it away from you. You're in avoid mode when you distract yourself from a problem or try to "numb out" in front of the TV. Most of the time avoiding is unconscious; you just get interested in something else or want to chill out and be interested in nothing at all. But sometimes it is a purposeful attempt to shut out another person. Whether it is purposeful or not, your partner's avoidance will have a negative effect on the relationship if you perceive it as shutting you out. (Note: Your partner is far more likely to recognize that he or she might be inadvertently avoiding you than to agree that he or she is stonewalling or being cold, distant, rejecting, thoughtless, or inconsiderate.)

Attack means turning negative energy *against* someone. In attack mode you want to devalue, harm, incapacitate, or destroy. Attack mode can also include coercion or manipulation. You're in attack mode when you have the impulse, unconscious or otherwise, to take someone "down a peg"; put him "in his place"; or show that you are superior in knowledge, skill, talent, size, strength, stamina, sensitivity, creativity, or originality. Attack mode lowers other people's value by dismissing their perspectives or undermining their confidence. It is important to note that you can be in attack mode even when using a soft, kind voice, if your intent is any of the above. In fact, you don't even have to say anything; it can just be an attitude. Here are some examples.

Women, imagine that your partner just got home from work and is sitting in his favorite chair reading the paper. You want to talk to him, and he's engrossed in reading.

- In *approach* mode you might simply hold a positive attitude and do something else until he's finished his routine of reading the paper. Or you might go sit near him and enjoy the quiet time together and let him share any interesting articles with you. You could even pick up the sections he's not reading and enjoy the activity together.
- In *attack* mode you might say (in your kind voice), "Let's go run those errands." Even though this sounds positive, the underlying message is that his needs are less important than yours, plus you have interrupted his routine, and you know how important that is to him.

Other attack modes might include criticizing ("How can you sit there and read the paper with so many things to be done?") or judging (huffing around, thinking negative thoughts). The list is endless.

* In *avoid* mode you might leave him sitting there reading the paper while you walk down to the purple martin house to check to see if you have any new birds, knowing this is something he likes to do with you. In this way you deliberately leave him out and exclude him from a connecting behavior.

Men, imagine that your partner is complaining that you don't listen to her.

* In *approach* mode you might say, "You're right. I get distracted or tired. I need to listen to you more." (You probably believe this but are afraid to tell her, because it means that you will have to listen to her all night. But it rarely works out that way. She wants to talk to gain connection. Once you're connected, her desire to talk diminishes and she will actually talk less!)

* In *attack* mode you might say (in your kind voice), "I listened to you last night. Tonight I have to pay the bills." This might sound reasonable, but you are intimating that she is not *worth* listening to, and that is almost certainly what she will hear.

* In *avoid* mode you might pretend not to hear her or try to distract yourself with the kids or the TV.

As a general rule, approach *reduces* fear and shame. Avoid and attack *increase* fear and shame.

Besides the fact that it is easier to recognize and change motivations than to figure out feelings, there is another compelling reason to focus on motivations. From early childhood we happen to be extremely accurate in reading whether people are in approach, avoid, or attack mode, but we are seldom accurate in reading their thoughts and feelings. Oh, we know they are thinking and feeling something, but we aren't often right about what. In contrast, you know pretty well whether they're approaching, avoiding, or attacking. Information about the motivation of other people is processed first in the amygdala, the organ in the brain that mediates basic emotion, *before* it is processed in the neocortex, where thought and language originate. The amygdala is a primitive structure in the brain that is common to all mammals and fully developed by the age of three. That is why very young children are highly accurate in reading approach, avoid, attack and why even your dog and cat can do it without having to talk about it.

Why Your Goals and Intentions Don't Really Count

Motivation differs from *goals* and *intentions* in important ways. You may have a *goal* of getting your partner to understand the family's financial situation and the *intention* of persuading him or her to cooperate with a certain budget. But if you are not in *approach* mode, you will naturally ignore or blow off your partner's perspective—it won't occur to you to pay attention to it while you're busy trying to explain your point of view. Feeling disregarded, your partner will get defensive and won't listen to you. Then you're likely to undermine, ignore, or devalue his or her perspective, implying that any competent and intelligent person would see things the way you do. Only in approach mode do you have any chance of fulfilling your goals and intentions.

Your partner responds almost exclusively to your motivations and hardly ever to your goals and intentions. When reacting to your avoid or attack mode your partner, children, and people in general are unlikely even to notice your goals and intentions and even less likely to care about them. People respond to the emotional tone of your motivation—what it *feels* like on the receiving end. Avoid and attack feel devaluing. That's why your attempts to clarify your goals and intentions will always fail, *unless* you change your motivation to approach, to wanting to understand and appreciate his or her perspective rather than influence, control, or manipulate it.

Talking and Motivation

As a general rule, talking to a woman puts her in approach mode. But when a woman starts talking to a man, he can easily slip into avoid mode, even if he wasn't in it when she started. First, there is the abrupt change, which, as we explored in Part I, floods him with cortisol. On top of that it invokes the male dread of failure because he expects to hear you tell him something that he is doing wrong. This general rule of male-female motivation means that you must have understanding and appreciation of your partner's perspective. Fortunately, approach modes that include attempts to understand and appreciate are almost as contagious to our partners as avoid and attack modes. In other words, if you are interested in your partner, he or she is likely to become interested in you. But if you dismiss, avoid, or devalue, what do you think will be the likely response?

Here's the big bonus of focusing on your motivations: You do not have to worry about figuring out whatever convoluted feelings you have. All you need to do is ask yourself these questions:

"Are my actions moving us toward connection or away from it?"

"Is my behavior consistent with my core values (the most important things to and about me as a person and as a partner)?"

"Is my motivation to approach, avoid, or attack?"

Be Sure *He's* Approachable

Understanding motivations sheds light on a common response we hear from women, which is: "I tell him, but he doesn't listen." Our experience reveals a slight difference. You tell him when he's not listening! **Bottom line: Don't talk to a man like you talk to a woman.** Before you assume that you have his attention, take time to make sure he is in approach mode.

Talking *puts* a woman in approach mode because women bond around talking. Moreover, talking doesn't interrupt a woman if she's engaged in another activity. She can listen even if she's fully engaged in something else, because her brain is uniquely designed for multitasking. She can continue with the taks and carry on a conversation at the same time. Men are different. Their brains are designed to focus on one thing at a time, and they are socialized in many ways to take advantage of that "single-mindedness." When you start talking to a man, he has to choose between completing the task at hand and talking to you. If he is fully engrossed he may not even hear you, especially if you are talking in a matter-of-fact way. If you are anxious or upset, his arousal alarm will go off and he'll shift his focus. But, remember, an abrupt change in your fear level will activate his defensive instincts—all you'll get is anger or irritability. Better to respect his space and make sure he is in approach mode before you initiate any meaningful exchange.

Be Sure *She's* Approachable

Many men we have worked with give up too easily when trying to make connection with their wives. Women are great at multitasking, which means they usually have a lot of things going at the same time. You might try to engage her when she's cooking, watching the kids, thinking about the laundry, the project at work, and the upcoming meeting with your son's math teacher. The best way to approach her when she's got so many pots on the burner is to offer *help*.

Try this exercise to check your motivation. Think of a specific time when you found that she was not approachable and circle the italicized words that apply.

1. Did you try to *understand* her perspective, *ignore* it, or *devalue* (criticize) it? (What *was* her perspective?)
2. Did you *respect* her opinion, *ignore* it, or *devalue* it?
3. Did you try to persuade her by *increasing* her confidence or by *decreasing* it? (For example, if you want to discuss paying bills, you would tell her that you are having trouble with the budget and ask if she can help you figure it out. That would increase her confidence in finding a solution and make her more approachable. On the other hand, implying that any idiot would see it the way you do will have the opposite effect.)

Checklist of Motivations
Toward Your Partner

Think of an average weekend and check the top two words that most often describe you in each of the three motivation categories:

APPROACH		AVOID		ATTACK	
Connect	☐	Ignore	☐	Criticize	☐
Protect	☐	Manipulate	☐	Judge	☐
Nurture	☐	Control	☐	Devalue	☐
Encourage	☐	Withdraw	☐	Reject	☐
Appreciate	☐	Dismiss	☐	Demand	☐
Understand	☐	Disregard	☐	Coerce	☐
Influence/ guide	☐	Overlook	☐	Dominate	☐
Negotiate/ cooperate	☐	Deny	☐	Threaten	☐
Request behavior change	☐	Distract	☐	Abuse (verbally or physically)	☐
Engage	☐	Sulk	☐	Punish	☐
Help/support	☐				
Collaborate/ cooperate	☐				

Now write down how you think your partner *perceives* your motivations. In other words, if you think you're encouraging or engaging, does he think you're coercing or does she think you're controlling?

APPROACH	AVOID	ATTACK
My motivations:	My motivations:	My motivations:
How he or she perceives them:	How he or she perceives them:	How he or she perceives them:

To get a little more specific about your motivations, we now invite you to look at particular aspects of your relationship that require your energy and attention. Complete the following survey to get a reading on how approachable you are.

How Approachable Are You?

In relationships, connection occurs when you are both approachable (in approach mode). Use the scale below to describe your motivation level within the last six months regarding each area listed.

APPROACH MODE			AVOID OR ATTACK MODE				
7	6	5	4	3	2	1	0
7 to 5			*Approach* means open, available, cooperative, interested, accessible.				
4 to 0			*Avoid* means unwilling to participate, uninterested, shut down, uncooperative.				
4 to 0			*Attack* means get angry, become defensive, criticize, demean, judge, resent.				

The lower the number, the more defended and uncooperative you are. If you choose a 4 or lower, circle the mode you use, avoid or attack. If you use both, circle both. (Example: If you refuse your partner's sexual advances or ignore his or her needs, under the category "being a good sex partner" you would circle a 4 or lower, depending on how long you have refused or how angry or insensitive your response has been.)

Circle the number that represents your behavior regarding the following activities:

1. Budgeting and spending

APPROACH MODE			AVOID OR ATTACK MODE				
7	6	5	4	3	2	1	0

2. Participating fairly in household chores

APPROACH MODE			AVOID OR ATTACK MODE				
7	6	5	4	3	2	1	0

3. Giving and receiving *nonsexual* affection

APPROACH MODE			AVOID OR ATTACK MODE				
7	6	5	4	3	2	1	0

4. Showing an ongoing interest in my partner

APPROACH MODE			AVOID OR ATTACK MODE				
7	6	5	4	3	2	1	0

5. Being a good sex partner

APPROACH MODE			AVOID OR ATTACK MODE				
7	6	5	4	3	2	1	0

6. Making my partner's needs a priority

APPROACH MODE			AVOID OR ATTACK MODE				
7	6	5	4	3	2	1	0

7. Being romantic

APPROACH MODE			AVOID OR ATTACK MODE				
7	6	5	4	3	2	1	0

8. Being interested in my partner's interests, hobbies, work

APPROACH MODE			AVOID OR ATTACK MODE				
7	6	5	4	3	2	1	0

9. Creating an emotionally safe environment in our relationship

APPROACH MODE			AVOID OR ATTACK MODE				
7	6	5	4	3	2	1	0

10. Regulating my negative thoughts and emotions

APPROACH MODE			AVOID OR ATTACK MODE				
7	6	5	4	3	2	1	0

11. Being faithful and trustworthy

APPROACH MODE			AVOID OR ATTACK MODE				
7	6	5	4	3	2	1	0

12. Being a good friend to my partner

APPROACH MODE			AVOID OR ATTACK MODE				
7	6	5	4	3	2	1	0

13. Being enjoyable to live with

APPROACH MODE			AVOID OR ATTACK MODE				
7	6	5	4	3	2	1	0

14. Being an active, supportive member of our family

APPROACH MODE			AVOID OR ATTACK MODE				
7	6	5	4	3	2	1	0

15. Making communication easy

APPROACH MODE			AVOID OR ATTACK MODE				
7	6	5	4	3	2	1	0

There are several ways you can interpret your scores on this survey. Just a glance at the numbers you circled will give you a reading on how approachable you are. However, you might want to look at individual areas to begin changing your motivation from avoid or attack to approach. Simply increasing the amount of time you spend in approach mode while decreasing avoid and attack motivations will certainly improve your relationship without talking about it.

Change Comes from Your Core Values

The big question is: How do you switch into approach mode when you have negative feelings about your partner? You do it from your core values. You make a choice to approach by deciding what is more important to you: ignoring or devaluing your partner on the one hand or improving, appreciating, connecting, and protecting on the other. Remember, your bad feelings come from the degree of disconnection you experience. In your core values, your gut-level compassion for the most important adult in your life will take over and lead you to the closer connection you both want.

The next chapter is written by Steven specifically for men, to help them appreciate their enormous power to create the kind of loving relationship they want. Best of all, they can do it without becoming women!

thirteen

man to man

How to Strengthen Your Relationship Without Becoming a Woman

This chapter is written by Steven for men.

One of the happiest experiences of my life as a therapist was when I realized that the men I worked with could use what they believed was the most important thing about them—their deep desire to protect their loved ones—to improve their relationships and make their wives happy, without having to talk about it and without feeling like they had to become more like women. The key is in the male attachment style: protect and connect.

Protection of loved ones is a survival instinct. It's so important to the continued existence of the human species that the primary function of anger and aggression in humans is not *self*-protection, as you might think. Anger and aggression developed in humans primarily for the protection of loved ones. If you doubt that, imagine what would make you the angriest and most aggressive—if I were to attack *you* or your wife and children. Instinctual protection of loved ones *overrides* self-protection; it will make you risk your life to protect those you love. You might not step in front of a bullet to protect your wife and child if you *thought* about it, but you would likely act on the instinct to protect *without* thinking about it.

It works the same way among males of other social species. Males are not in the pack just for reproduction—sperm donation by itself does not require emotional investment in the welfare of the group. The main purpose of males in social organizations is *protection* of the group from predators. That is why the males of most species of mammals have greater muscle mass, more efficient blood flow to the muscles and organs, bigger fangs and claws, quicker reflexes, longer strides, more electrical activity in the central nervous system, and a thicker amygdala—the organ in the limbic system that activates emergency response. Even in those species where the females are the primary hunters, as in lions, the males assume the role of protectors of the group. In all social animals, the males form a defensive perimeter to fend off attacks by other animals, while the females gather the young and try to hide within the circle of protection.

Although the instinct to protect seems to be embedded in the genes of all social mammals, it is strongest in humans. I'd like to think that this is due to our sense of morality, but it is probably due to the fact that our young are helpless and vulnerable for a much longer time. Animals with weaker social bonds are on their feet and running ten minutes after birth. As you go up the food chain, the young are helpless for increasingly longer periods and therefore require stronger emotional bonding with their mothers or parents. By the time you get to humans—well, these days our young are dependent until they're about thirty-five.

The survival importance of the instinct to protect gives it dominance over the masculine sense of self-value. We automatically suffer low self-value when we fail to protect our loved ones, no matter how successful we might be in other areas of life. (Imagine the emotional fate of a world-class CEO who lets go of his child's hand in traffic.) However, your self-value will be intact, even if you fail at work, as long as you protect your loved ones. Research shows that getting fired is tolerable for those men more attuned to the protection of their families than to their own egos. These men tend to search immediately for another job as a means of putting food on the table, while those who take failure at work as an assault on their egos will face weeks of despair or depression before they get up the ego strength to job hunt once again.

Protect and Connect

The relationship style of most men is *protect and connect.* You are more likely to feel emotionally connected to your partner if you feel that you can successfully protect her. If you *don't* feel that you can adequately protect her, for whatever reason, you are likely to feel uncomfortable with—if not *unworthy* of—an emotional connection to her. You're likely to get angry or withdraw when she asks for more closeness.

Beware of feeling unworthy of connection. Men who feel unworthy of connection are often worse than just bad husbands and fathers. Science has known for a long time that emotional connection inhibits violence and that disconnection is a cause of violence. Violent criminals usually lack what sociologists call a *stake in the community*—job, positive neighborhood connections, religious affiliation, and satisfying intimate and parental relationships. Serial killers and terrorists never have close relationships with their children. Historically, armies wanted soldiers *before* they had children, and when they did have them, they were kept isolated from them. In other social animals, males connected to the pack are more cooperative and serve as significant *protectors,* while those driven from it become rogue predators, often picking off weaker members of the pack in stealth.

The steep rise in domestic violence since the 1960s directly parallels the decline of fatherhood in America. When fathers are marginalized as protectors of their families, they are more likely to struggle for power and control over their wives or girlfriends. They compensate for failure to protect with dominance. My experience with thousands of court-ordered domestic violence offenders tells me that when fathers are more involved in the lives of their children, they are unlikely to hurt *any* woman. While still developing our intervention for domestic violence some sixteen years ago, we took a group of sixteen young men (mean age twenty-two) in Prince Georges County, Maryland. All these young men had at least two children from previous relationships and had been ordered by the courts into treatment for abuse of their current partners. (At that time, there was only one agency offering domestic violence services, and it had a very long waiting list.) As is too often the case with young, unmarried fathers, none of these guys had a relationship with his children or their mothers. We gave them a brief course called "Compassionate Parenting" that raised their awareness of the emotional worlds of their children, particularly their need to have fathers who cared about them. The young men who got more involved in the lives of their children completely stopped abusing their girlfriends without direct intervention for domestic violence. The normal recidivism rate for unmarried men of this age group was over 60 percent, *after* domestic violence intervention. In our group it was 0.

The Failure to Protect Formula:
Instinct to *Protect* + Fear of *Failure* = *Control*

Research shows that when women express vulnerable emotions (and they usually do it in the form of complaints) men try to tell them what to do to *fix* the problem. When their partners respond negatively to feeling controlled—as they almost always do—the same men who start out trying to help get disgusted and wash their hands of the "whole mess," as in, "Do whatever you want—just leave me alone!" They feel just as rejected and frustrated as their partners, who interpret their behavior as *My way or the highway!*

The majority of men who have reacted this way to their partners' requests for closeness—even when those requests sound like complaints, nagging, or indictments—do not *mean* to control them or reject them if they won't follow the "higher wisdom of masculine counsel." These poor guys, *me* included, just try to avoid the pain of failure to protect.

The tragedy is this: By giving in to resentment, anger, or withdrawal, we cut ourselves off from the most important thing about us, which is our desire to protect loved ones. The great test of masculinity in our modern era is not going into the woods and eating bugs to prove we can overcome our fear in a bold display of our survival skills; it's learning to protect the women in our lives without trying to control them.

Her Complaint Is Really a Plea for Connection

Protection in committed relationships is *different* from protection in dating. The battle cry is no longer "to the rescue" or "I'll fix this for you." The key now is *maintenance, empowerment, assistance,* and *friendship.* Our partners complain when we fail to do these things, not to criticize us (even though it can sure sound like criticism) but to gain connection. And we have to respond *protectively* to their pleas, even when they sound like complaints.

Protection involves caring about her *emotions* more than the *content* of what she says. You can disagree with the content, as long as you value *her.* If she feels valued, she will feel protected and connected, even when you disagree with her. If you value her, you will feel protective and connected, even if she disagrees with you. You *know* how to do this; it's precisely how you forged your bond in the beginning of your relationship. The difference now is that you are more reactive to her surface emotions and less sensitive to her underlying vulnerability. **If she nags or is resentful, angry, or too busy to acknowledge your existence, she is anxious about something. Connection will lower her anxiety, but your defensiveness, withdrawal, or criticism will raise it.**

Love Is Following the Instinct to Protect and Connect

There was a time when your partner, before she *was* your partner, talked to you about various things that made her feel anxious or insecure. You most likely responded with a sense of protectiveness. You knew intuitively that she was upset. If she felt disregarded, you paid more attention to her. If she felt unimportant, you showed her that she was important to you. If she felt accused, you reassured her. If she felt guilty, you helped her feel better. If she felt devalued, you valued her more. If she felt rejected, you accepted her; if she felt powerless, you tried to empower her; if she felt inadequate, you helped her appreciate her competence; and if she felt unlovable, you loved her more. You did all this out of a natural desire to protect the person you loved.

You fell in love because you were able to connect, and you were able to connect because you felt protective. It started to go wrong when you began to see your impulse to take care of her, which made you feel *great* while dating, as costing too much time or money in a committed love relationship. You probably had good reasons for starting to feel that way, but as long as you feel that way, you will not find viable solutions to time and money problems. In other words, **things will certainly get worse until you decide to be protective of your partner's fear as you used to be; and in the long run, this will cost far less in time and money than a disconnected relationship and divorce.**

Of course, this switch in how you reacted to her anxiety was confusing to her, to say the least. She was doing the same thing that used to invoke your protectiveness—worrying or expressing needs—but now she provoked your anger and resentment. It's as if once you got married you expected that she would never again feel bad, or at least not show that she did. When she did show it, you interpreted her complaints as an indictment of *your* failure as a protector.

Why Protection Is So Much Harder Now

The protective instinct was much easier to follow in the days when it developed in early humans. Then it was limited to things like putting a big rock by the cave entrance so the saber-toothed tiger couldn't get in and fighting off predators and scavengers to bring home a few scraps of food to feed loved ones and some fur to keep them warm. *Protect* meant keeping them from harm and severe deprivation.

Your instinct to protect your wife is the same now as our distant ancestors had then—to protect your mate from fear of harm, isolation, and deprivation. But cavemen could feel okay about themselves as protectors as long as they kept their families alive. That's the key word: *alive.* If you failed as a protector or provider *then,* it meant certain *death.* That's why the instinct to protect provokes intense anxiety in modern men. Failure to provide a necklace is not going to kill your partner, but it will give you a dread of failure that taps directly into the survival instincts we inherited from our ancestors, for whom failure meant death.

You resent your partner for wanting the necklace because she makes you feel like a failure as a provider. Not that you *are* a failure as a provider—it has nothing to do with rational judgment; the dread of failure rarely rises to conscious. I have one client who is a billionaire and enormously generous to his wife when they feel connected, but when they do not, he gets remarkably upset about her spending, which, in the course of their relationship, has never amounted to a month's interest on his fortune. And of course when they are disconnected, she spends more.

Your partner absolutely must feel safe and secure at all times and emotionally connected to you *a lot* of the time. When she does not feel safe, secure, and connected, she suffers unconscious fear of isolation, which, in turn, stimulates her fear of deprivation, which means she is likely to shop more (for herself and others), eat more, drink more, or consume more. Her increased level of shopping and consuming stimulates your dread of failure as a provider. If you respond by criticizing or withdrawing—*disconnecting*—she will likely spend more as you embark on the downward spiral to divorce.

Love Is Cheap, Guilt Is Expensive

You must understand that your partner is not *causing* your dread of failure, although she can certainly remind you that you have it. For instance, you will not feel better if she gives in and denies herself the necklace she really wants, because on some deep, irrational level, *you* think you *should* get it for her. And *that's* what you have to transform, the conflict within *you*. If you rely on *her* to transform your dread of failure, you won't want her even to *want* it. She will sin *in thought,* if she does. To protect yourself from the dread of failure her desires stimulate in you, you'll withdraw from her. Her wants and desires will become alien to you, and eventually you'll feel like you're living with a stranger. You'll feel like little more than a paycheck, and she'll feel like all you want her for is sex. **If you want to feel like more than a paycheck, you have to *behave* like more than a paycheck.** You have to connect with her, make her feel safe and secure, and provide emotional support for her growth and development.

Why Sex Is Such a Hot Button

I became a pubescent male just before the Kinsey report on female sexuality was published. At that time, we were almost embarrassed to fantasize about having sex with girls because it seemed so selfish—they couldn't possibly get anything out of it. And if they would do it just for us, when there wasn't anything in it for them, what would they demand in return? Would we have to go shopping with them? Talk to them about girl stuff? Where would it all end?

Then we found out that women really *do* like sex, but that we have to do it *well.* Boy, did that open up a can of worms! Dr. Kinsey published the first scientific study to reveal that for women, sex was a lot more complicated, required considerably more preparation, and took a lot longer to be satisfying. We didn't just have to worry about getting a woman into bed; now we really had to worry about what to do with her once she was there.

They called this male worry "performance anxiety," a phrase that appeared regularly in the popular media, usually with the word *new* in front of it, as in the "new performance anxiety." It wasn't really new; the male dread of failure as a lover had been around forever but had been limited to the woes of erectile dysfunction and premature ejaculation. Those were bad enough, but now we had to learn foreplay, get it up and keep it up long enough and with enough "technique" for her to have an earth-moving orgasm. It was one thing to be rejected by a woman who didn't like sex—after all, it was asking a lot of her anyway—but quite another to be rejected because you're just not good enough as a lover. One amusing indication of this threat to the male ego was the depiction in comic-horror movies of the rejecting, sexually dissatisfied woman.

Thousands of books have appeared over the years reinforcing the male performance myth by giving tips on techniques that could make the earth move for her. Well, here's free advice on how to be a great lover: Make an emotional connection with her. The sexiest thing you can do is also the most healing to your relationship: Cultivate a high level of compassion for your partner.

Think about a time when you wanted to have sex and she didn't. It's probably not hard to recall how you felt. But for her it's not a question of shame or humiliation; it's fear or anxiety. Think for a moment about how her anxiety about the issue might have made it difficult to "get into the mood." Was she afraid that you didn't care about her feelings, that you might leave her or reject her if she didn't want to have sex? Think of how you could reassure her with sympathy and caring. You could rub her shoulders, kiss her forehead, and tell her you love her even though you're not going to have sex right now. Another idea is to take over one of her regular responsibilities to help relieve her stress. Many women say that this is the best aphrodisiac.

Now think about a time when *she* wanted sex and you didn't. Her anxiety would be about her attractiveness and whether you might leave her. How can you reassure her with sympathy and caring? You certainly don't want to reject her. You could pleasure her sexually using manual or oral stimulation.

Compassion as the Ultimate Protection

The secret of a better sex life and a better relationship is to be more compassionate and aware of the fear and anxiety hidden beneath your partner's worries, busyness, requests, complaints, demands, and nagging. I'm talking about a gut-level sensitivity to her vulnerability, even when she is not showing it. This is especially important if she seems to be accusing you of something. It's natural to feel defensive when you're being accused. But the implication when you defend yourself is that you don't care about her hurt—you care only about defending your own ego. The trick is to respond automatically to the vulnerability under the complaint, and then disagree with the accusation. Most of the time, when you are sympathetic to her hurt, she'll withdraw or at least modify her accusation. Consider the following examples. First, we'll hear the common defensive response—I'd be rich if I had a dime each time I heard some variation on this one in my office.

"You're *never* home," Sally said when Jack came in late from work. "If you think I'm going to warm up your dinner, forget it. I'm not your maid."

"I came home on time two days this week," he countered. "You *know* how much work we have."

"Oh, two days out of five. I guess I should consider myself lucky. I really wanted to get married to have a husband forty percent of the time."

"Why should I bother to come home when I have to put up with *this!*"

You get the picture. They could go on like that all night—and sometimes they have—going back and forth in vain attempts to decide who was right. Should he work less and spend more time with the family or should she be more understanding that he's working *for* the family?

Of course they're *both* right. But it's not the either-or proposition they make it out to be. She *would* be more understanding of his hard work if she felt connected to him when he *was* home. The problem is that he feels guilty for not being home and blames it on her, which makes him insensitive to the fact that she misses him. Think about it, she's complaining because she misses him and wants to be with him.

Now here's how it looks when compassion overrides defensiveness.

"You're never home," Sally accuses.

Jack puts his briefcase down and hugs her warmly. "I miss you when I have to work so much. You deserve more attention. I wish we didn't have so much work."

"Do you want me to warm up your dinner?" she asks.

Not only does compassion sensitize you to the vulnerability under her resentment and anger but also it *calms* both of you with the soothing connection of attachment. This is what they *both* wanted in the countless defensive dialogues they had previously—to feel calm and connected. Substitute compassion for defensiveness, and you'll find that you won't have to be defensive at all.

Most of your resentment comes from feeling that you are failing your partner as an emotional protector. There is only one thing that will make you feel successful as an emotional protector: *compassion*.

Here are the key points for exercising compassion for your partner in an argument:

- Understand your own perspective, rather than merely opposing hers. (Example: You both want to send your kids to private schools, but she complains that you have to work overtime a lot to afford it. Instead of attacking her position, think of why it is important for you to send the kids to private school and to work extra to do it.)
- Identify any defensive reaction you might have had. (Example: I got angry and wanted her to shut up.)
- Identify how your vulnerability to failure, shame, loss of status, or inadequacy are involved. (Example: I don't make enough money to send the kids to private school and have enough time left over to be

a good father. I'm failing as a provider, protector, partner, and parent. On top of that, I'm too tired and stressed to be a good lover.)

- Identify her perspective, as *she* would relate it. Don't edit it or give your perspective of it. Try to use the words she would use to describe it. (Example: If you really wanted to, you could make more time for me and the kids.)

- Identify her deepest fear. (Example: When I get stressed she feels like I don't want to be in contact with her, and that makes her afraid that I might leave her and she won't be able to send the kids to private school or buy nice things for them.)

- Increase your connection, which means reducing your shame and her fear at the same time. (Example: I would let her know that her happiness and the kids' well-being are the reasons I work so hard *and* that I want to be more connected to her when I am home.)

Some guys try to avoid compassion out of fear that it might be interpreted as weakness and lead to their greatest dread: "being taken advantage of." **If you are thinking in terms of "weakness" or exploitation, your relationship is already choking with resentment and you are probably in a chronic state of powerlessness.**

What an irony! To avoid feelings that might seem "weak," we make ourselves completely *powerless* and unable to make our relationships better, while desperately hoping against hope that they don't get worse. We're not *that* stupid about power and weakness, are we? Well, it has nothing to do with intelligence. It has everything to do with a contradiction in the cultural definition of *masculinity*. Taking the Wimp Test below should make the point. Better yet, read the questions and your answers out loud.

The Wimp Test

Write "real man" next to those statements you think describe someone of courage, or "wimp" next to those statements you think describe a wimp.

1. He's *afraid* to admit to himself what he really feels. _____
2. He's *afraid* to take responsibility for himself and blames others for what he thinks, feels, and does. _____
3. He's *afraid* to internalize power, and instead relies on other people to make him feel powerful and to make him feel good or bad. _____
4. He's *afraid* to be intimate. _____
5. He's *afraid* to be compassionate. _____
6. He *hides* behind resentment or anger because he's *afraid* to feel like a failure. _____

Answer "yes" or "no"

7. Is a real man *afraid* to feel hurt? Does he *need* to cover up his feelings with anger, resentment, withdrawal, or aggression? _____
8. Would a real man hurt his wife's feelings to keep from feeling a few seconds of rejection or disrespect or devaluation? _____

The Wimp Test reframes traditional macho values in terms of fear, to show you the contradiction in cultural definitions of masculinity. Most cultures describe manliness as *courage*—the ability to withstand pain and overcome fear, to protect what you most value. Yet popular images of masculinity often imply terror of emotions. The Marlboro Man rides alone into the desert to smoke himself to death, because speaking to a woman might cause an emotion he won't be able to handle. Talk about powerlessness!

Genuine Power

Power is not just the ability to do something or to get someone else to do something. For instance, you have the power to drive your car into the side of a building, and you might even be able to coerce your partner into doing the same. But would you be powerful if you did that? Obviously, you'd be stupid if you did that. Shooting yourself in the foot is not power.

Power is the ability to act in your long-term best interest. It is behaving according to what you believe to be the most important things about you. Your compassion moves you to improve, appreciate, connect, and protect, while your resentment makes you devalue by avoidance or attack. Which will be in your best interest and, therefore, more powerful in your relationship?

Compassion is power.

The Compassion Paradox: If Available *Whenever* Needed, It's Rarely Needed

Research shows that when people—men *and* women—feel secure that compassion and support will be there if they need it, they are far more independent. Worry that it *won't* be available when needed creates a *deprivation mentality*. You can think of deprivation mentality in the following way. If you haven't eaten for over a week, are you likely to hold out for a gourmet dinner and eat it with your napkin in place and cut up your food carefully? Or will you shovel whatever food you can get into your mouth as fast as you can? You're likely to resemble a hungry wolf more than a well-mannered diner. Well, the last thing you want is for your partner to be as hungry as a wolf for emotional support. That will make her think about her emotional needs *all* the time and want more and more attention, until it seems to you that she can never get enough. The trick is applying *preventive* compassion in *small doses,* so that she knows it will always be there when she needs it. Once she knows that, she will hardly ever need it.

Using Shame as a Motivator—
Stepping Up to the Plate

The problem of always acting to avoid feeling shame is that it nullifies your own early warning system, which makes it likely that you're going to get burned. Think of your shame as an alarm telling you that you need to be true to the most important things about you. As soon as you are, you start to feel much better. Use the following grid for practicing this crucial skill.

Copy this grid and keep it with you to practice whenever you can. The goal is to turn the first hint of shame avoidance (I want to run, etc.) into a signal to step up to the plate and hit a home run of understanding, appreciation, protection, and connection. The first few times you do it will be difficult—you'll be sailing against the winds of habit. But it gets easier with each repetition. Before you know it, the experience of shame is but a faint shadow in the history of your emotional past.

Go back and read the grid again right now—you can't read it too much!

| Whenever she criticizes, complains, gets angry, irritable, resentful, etc. | I feel annoyed, angry, resentful, tired, fed up, etc. | Then I want to run, crawl into a hole, shout, slam doors, etc. | But if I force myself to understand that her fear of isolation, deprivation, or harm comes from her desire to love me and to feel loved by me, | I want to protect her, without trying to control her, to let her know that I care about how she feels, to appreciate her, and to connect with her mentally, even if I can't connect with her physically at that moment. |

Note: If you or your partner feels that you might need extra work in the area of anger, you can refer to www.compassionpower.com. Anger can be an especially difficult problem if you've ever suffered a head injury that caused you to lose consciousness or if you consume more than one or two alcoholic drinks per day. The approach of this book is more for prevention than for putting out fires, to hurricane proof your relationship so that it can withstand occasional storms. It should have the effect of reducing the frequency and severity of the storms. If it does not, you may need additional help with healing the hurt that causes your anger.

The next chapter shows how to incorporate protect-and-connect behavior into your daily routine, which will make it much easier to respond protectively to your partner's fears.

the power love formula

Four and Three-Quarter Minutes a Day to a Powerful Relationship

We have saved the best for last. If you've made it this far, you have earned the right to the Power Love Formula, which is simple yet profound. The formula has four steps, which, when practiced routinely, will create love beyond words. The decision to use the formula is in your hands; this means that **deep emotional connection is a personal choice** you can make beginning right now. That's right: you can *choose* to feel connected to your partner, just as you *choose* to feel disconnected; and, in general, you will like yourself more when you choose to feel connected and feel bad (resentful, depressed, anxious, bored, numb, or angry) when you choose to feel disconnected. And here's more good news. You can use the Power Love Formula *on your own*. You don't need your partner's cooperation. He or she doesn't even have to know you are doing it. What *will* be known will be that your emotional demeanor will have taken on a new positive dimension because of your choice to be deeply connected. Here are the four steps.

The Power Love Formula

1. Fix your partner firmly in your heart during four crucial times of the day.

2. Hug your partner six times a day for six seconds.
3. Hold positive thoughts about your relationship.
4. Make a contract to hand out love with compassion and generosity.

The key to big change lies in small, everyday emotions. The idea here is to ensure that thoughts and behaviors that foster connection are a part of your daily routine. The Power Love Formula takes less than five minutes a day and will certainly strengthen your relationship. Here are the details for each step.

1. Fix your partner firmly in your heart during four crucial times of the day.

We love love songs because they express emotional connection in a way that most of us are unable to do. Occasional love songs are nice but unnecessary for a stronger connection. What *is* necessary is developing a routine that includes holding the most important person in your life close to your heart. To do this, we ask you to come up with a brief gesture that acknowledges your partner's significance. It can be repeating a phrase like "You are so important to me" or "You give value to my life." It can be simply reaching out your hand for a brief touch or making eye contact. Whatever you come up with should, of course, come from your heart.

Once you decide what your heart gesture will be, practice it routinely during the four crucial times of each day: 1. when you wake up, 2. before you leave home, 3. when you come back home, and 4. before you go to sleep. Here's why these times are crucial. Research shows that low-arousal emotions lead one into another in a more or less continuous flow, something like a stream that starts in the morning and extends throughout the day. If your first emotion of the day is positive, it is more likely that your next one will also be positive. And then it becomes more likely that the one after that will be positive, and still more likely that the next will be positive, and so on. In other words, emotional experience is not like flipping a coin, where the chances of heads or tails is always 50 percent, regardless of how many tosses you've made. Preceding emotions greatly influence subsequent ones, forming positive or negative streams that continue to gain momentum like a stream flowing downhill, until something good or bad in the environment changes them. Think about your best days. It's fairly certain that most of them started with a positive thought or gesture. If you start each day by holding your partner close to your heart, whether he or she knows it or not, it will start the flow of your emotions positively and greatly improve your relationship without talking. If you make these brief acknowledgments of your partner's importance, you will see within a few weeks that affirming your partner's value first thing in the morning is one of the best things you can do for your overall health and well-being.

Your second daily acknowledgment should occur before you leave the house in the morning. This sets the tone for the time the two of you will be apart. The third should happen when you return in the evening. Setting a positive tone for spending the prebedtime hours together will raise the comfort level of the whole household. Finally, right before you fall asleep, again, hold your partner close to your heart. This routine will sweeten your dreams and carry your love into the next morning.

2. Hug your partner six times a day for six seconds.

Hugs are usually the first thing to go when resentment takes over a relationship. Over time, failure to embrace becomes a formula for disaster. It's very simple: The less you touch, the more resentful you get. The following routine, which takes thirty-six seconds per day, is designed to reverse this downward spiral of a hugless relationship.

Hug your partner in a full-body embrace a minimum of six times a day, holding each hug for a minimum of six seconds. The six-times-six formula is not arbitrary. You probably do not hug more than once or twice a day now. Increasing that to six times a day will facilitate a new level of closeness. The six-second minimum for each hug recognizes that in the beginning some of those hugs will be forced. They can start out forced but will become genuine at about the fourth or fifth second, provided that you are still attached and not yet in the contempt stage of detachment. This kind of embrace increases serotonin levels to give a general calming effect that can even help to reduce appetite. Not a bad deal—you'll feel better in general and less edgy, irritable, and sad in particular, and maybe drop a pound or two in the process of feeling closer.

3. Hold positive thoughts about your relationship.

This is easy. At some point during your workday, as often as you can do it, stop for ten seconds to think positive thoughts about your partner. List three below:

_____

_____

_____

_____

_____

4. Make a contract to hand out love with compassion and generosity.

Make a contract stating "This is how I will show my love for you every day."

Keep it brief and simple, write it like a legal contract, and do it at an agreed-upon time *every* day. To structure your thinking, try completing this sentence: "If I loved him/her, I would . . ."

Examples:

* Look him in the eyes and tell him something about him that I really appreciate.
* Let her know how important she is to me.
* Allow myself to be comforted by him.
* Let her know how much I love to see her happy.
* Let him know that I believe in him.
* Show how my life is better because of her.

Here are some things that our clients have come up with. "I hereby agree to . . ."

* Speak in a kind voice.
* Light a candle for you.
* Bring you morning coffee in bed.
* Have your breakfast ready for you.
* Put a flower on your plate.
* Put a love note in a place where you will find it.

Use this form for your contract:

AGREEMENT

For value received (the privilege of loving you), I, _____, of _____ [street address], _____ [city], _____ [county], _____ [state], assign _____, of _____ [street address], _____ [city], _____ [county], _____ [state], to receive the following from me every day. I warrant that I will:

_____

_____

Implementing the Power Love Formula in a routine fashion will begin your journey to a love beyond words.

Contrary to what most people think, deep connection is not based on shared tastes—those things are fine, but they provide little depth to your re-lationships. Rather, deep connection is based on shared *values,* what is *most important* to you. Deeply connected couples share some of the follow-ing values:

* Love of some of the same people
* A capacity for some kind of spiritual connection (to something larger than the self, for example, God, nature, the cosmos, humanity, or political and social causes)
* A capacity to appreciate (though not necessarily the same things or in the same way): nature; human-made beauty (art, music, architecture, crafts, and so on); connection with certain groups of people (for example, neighbors, social, political, religious, school groups)
* A capacity to do compassionate things

Keep a list of the areas of deep connection—based on values—that you have now or might possibly develop in your relationship. Incorporate these shared values in the four steps of the Power Love Formula. When you hold your partner close to your heart during the crucial times of the day, remem-ber your shared values. When you are hugging your partner, remember your shared values; when you pause during the day to hang on to positive thoughts about your relationship, remember your shared values; and, fi-nally, use your shared values to hand out love to your partner with compas-sion and generosity. Practicing these routines will create an emotional lifeline.

Emotional Lifelines

Couples need emotional lifelines to stay connected, just as astronauts need lifelines during a space walk. Astronauts' lifelines provide an effective analogy because they afford maximum movement while providing lifesaving connection to the spacecraft. Emotional lifelines keep us connected to each other without tying us down.

Imagine a long and flexible lifeline connecting the two of you. No matter what you are doing or feeling, you remain connected. When you are in different locations, you are connected. When you are busy at work, you are connected. Even when you are angry at each other, you are connected. To remind yourself of the emotional lifeline connecting you and your partner, write the following sentence on a piece of paper and carry it with you wherever you go. Make a second copy and give it to your partner.

MY *LIFELINE* TO YOU

Me ────────────────────────────────────── **You**

These are the ways I am deeply connected to you. (Examples: *My life has more meaning because of you. We have a rich history together. When I am troubled, you are the one who comforts me.*)

_____

_____

_____

_____

_____

If you imagine yourself constantly connected by an invisible lifeline, your whole emotional demeanor around your partner will change for the better. Give your partner time to see that your new interest is not a passing whim, and he or she will almost certainly respond with appreciation and fondness. **The secret of feeling closer to your partner when you're together is to feel closer when you're apart.**

The simple, daily behaviors of your Power Love Formula will resensitize you to the emotional world of your partner. That by itself can restore your relationship to the level it was before the chain of resentment *desensitized* you to what you value most about him or her. This four-and-three-quarter-minute daily routine will also help you concentrate and perform better at work and, in general, create more value in your life. In other words, you will be rewiring your brain for more closeness. Through these brief rituals of connection that can be easily integrated into your daily routine, you will greatly improve your relationship without talking about it.

The Way Out When Fear and Shame Sneak Back In

Even with the best intentions and relationship skills in the world, you will not completely avoid triggering your partner's shame or fear. Fortunately, there is a way to quickly recover and reconnect when this happens and the inevitable disconnection occurs. The added bonus of reconnecting in the manner we suggest is that it greatly reduces the probability that you will do it again. We call the process the three R's:

RECOGNITION

REMORSE

REPAIR

Recognition

To recognize the behavior that triggered your partner's shame or fear you must be able to see your actions from your partner's point of view. This can be a humbling experience, because *the deepest form of hurt comes from hurting someone you love.* Acknowledging how your behavior—intentionally or unintentionally—hurt your partner will make you uncomfortable. Admitting fault is so difficult. No one wants to feel the agony that comes with knowing that you have caused someone else to suffer, especially someone you love, and yet the only way out of the pain is *through* the pain. You must be able to recognize the error of your actions or you cannot move on to reconnection. The truth is that even if you don't admit it, at some level you usually know when you hurt your partner. You can deny it and suppress your feelings, but the awareness will still be there. If you are a man, being aware of your insensitivity toward your partner will trigger your feelings of inadequacy, and you'll likely respond with anger or withdrawal. If you are a woman, becoming aware of your hurtful behavior will trigger your fear and you'll likely respond by invading his space, criticizing, or rejecting his love. The more anger, withdrawal, criticism, or rejection that exists in your relationship, the more you need recognition, remorse, and repair. And just because anger and criticism aren't being expressed overtly doesn't mean they don't exist. They can take many forms. Anger might show up as being sullen or irritable, being controlling, withdrawing, pouting, procrastinating, or being preoccupied or passive-aggressive. Criticism can take the form of having a judgmental attitude, being condescending, nit-picking, fault-finding, talking incessantly, insisting on your way, making up rules—the variations are endless. You can see why an unwillingness to recognize your hurtful behavior can drive a serious wedge between you and your partner.

The primary reason recognition is so important is: You are not going to change a behavior that you don't think exists. **As long as you deny your insensitive behavior that evokes fear or shame in your partner, you will not act differently.** This means fear, shame, and resentment will increase. In contrast, recognizing your mistakes induces compassion. That's right. If your partner comes to you with a heartfelt apology for the ways he or she has hurt you, your natural inclination is to be compassionate.

Recognizing you have hurt someone—gaining insight into your behavior—can come at the moment of transgression or any time after. Ideally, you catch yourself in the act before the wounded party has to call it to your attention. Remember Leticia and Bo who got their fear-shame dynamic going in full force on their way home from his high school reunion? Leticia didn't recognize that she had been insensitive to Bo's feelings until he struck out in anger. Had she realized it earlier, even while she was talking on the phone, she could have avoided further hurt by offering an apology—"I'm so sorry, I just answered that phone out of habit. I'm far more interested in what you have to say than any phone call." Likewise, Bo could have recognized Leticia's anxiety about ringing phones and not taken it so personally. When you recognize the error of your ways without being told, it goes a long way toward building trust, because a person who is aware of his or her mistakes is far less likely to hurt you in the same way again. In contrast, a person who will not recognize his or her offensiveness offers little hope for change and builds a wall of resentment.

Even if you recognize your insensitive behavior only after your partner has brought it to your attention, you can still move to steps two and three, remorse and repair. And by the way, it's never too late to acknowledge your faults. As you get to know yourself and your partner, the clearer it will be how you've made it hard for him or her to trust you. Don't wait for an argument to apologize. Just think how good you would feel if your partner came to you one day and said something as simple as "Thanks for putting up with me." Or if he were to make a big deal out of your anniversary, to acknowledge that hanging in there with him deserves recognition. Even if your insensitivity occurred a long time ago in a previous relationship, it is never too late to recognize the part you played in hurting the other person. Recognition might not be able to change the past, but you can avoid making the same mistake in the future. You might be surprised to find how apologizing to someone in your past will have a positive effect on your present relationships, especially if the apology is accompanied by the next step, remorse.

Remorse

Recognition without remorse is like saying you're sorry without *being* sorry or like taking a bath without soap. It's better than nothing but does little toward building trust or reducing shame and fear. Saying "I know I hurt you" without *feeling* what it is like to be hurt does little to reinstate connection. Talking the talk doesn't change how you walk the walk. It takes the corrective aspect of remorse to prevent the same insensitive behavior from happening again. True recognition—acknowledging how your behavior hurt your partner—will bring remorse unless you are just paying lip service—or you have the psyche of a hardened criminal.

The remorse you feel when you have hurt someone is a composite of sorrow, guilt, and regret. This feeling is uncomfortable for a reason. It hurts in order to get your attention, to remind you not to do it again. Once your brain connects your offensive behavior to the pain of remorse, you will avoid that behavior like the plague. In this way remorse is corrective. The desire to avoid the anguish brought on by remorse keeps us true to our word and on our best behavior. You cannot trust someone who feels no remorse because that person won't care if he or she hurts you.

Mature, healthy people feel remorse when they disappoint or hurt others, but it doesn't stop there. Remorse has to have legs. It must lead to repair, a corrective action, or it cannot heal the hurt.

Repair

If you have recognition and remorse but refuse to make amends, you come *close* to lasting reconciliation, but not close enough. For you have not yet defused the shame-fear bomb hidden in the cellars of your relationship. Coming close but falling short can even create more distance and resentment as your partner's hopes rise only to be dashed.

When you trigger your partner's fear or shame, both of you get hurt. Repair heals the hurt for both of you. We are a very forgiving species; recognition, remorse, and repair make it possible for your partner to forgive you and for you to forgive yourself.

Repair can come in many forms. For example, women are more inclined to make a verbal repair. This is fine as long as the talking is accompanied by a change in behavior. For repair to have legs, your actions have to look different. If Leticia said, "I am so sorry I made that phone call more important than you, please forgive me," then went right ahead and answered the phone during their next conversation, repair would not take place. If she offered a simple "I'm sorry," then proceeded to stay tuned to Bo instead of the phone, her repair would be effective. Because women tend to talk a problem to death, a man will be far more impressed with a change in her behavior instead of a litany of apologies. Even if her repair attempt is heartfelt and sincere, he will be skeptical and unforgiving until her behavior proves her words to be reliable. And by the way, she won't forgive herself until she changes her ways. It is much more effective to *talk less and do more*. Let your actions make the reconnection with your partner.

Men, on the other hand, tend to talk less, if at all, in their repair attempts. A man is far more likely to make repair with some new behavior like "Let's go for some ice cream" or "Can I help you do something?" A problem can occur if the woman is sitting around waiting for him to come to her with a female version of repair instead of acknowledging his new, improved behavior, which is his way of reconnecting. A common complaint we hear from men is "I make changes but she doesn't see them. All she sees is what I'm doing wrong." Imagine how discouraging it is to be making difficult attempts at repair with little or no acknowledgment from your partner.

Bottom line: Don't expect your partner to do it like you do it.

It's a lot easier to see your partner's offensive behavior than to see your own, and, contrary to popular belief, women are no better at it than men. In over fifty years of combined experience working with couples, neither Pat nor Steven has seen a woman bringing her partner to therapy to say, "I'm really hard to live with. Please help me be a better partner." Men and women struggle equally with the ability to see life through binocular vision. But if you can each practice recognition, remorse, and repair along with the Power Love Formula, focus on your motivation, and "step into the puddle" whenever necessary, you will find a love beyond words.

conclusion

If You Want to Love Big, You Have to Think Small

i t's nice to have occasional romantic weekends, intimate dinners, and great vacations, but don't expect them to have any long-lasting positive effects on your relationship. Unless accompanied by a loving *routine*, they are more likely to have a negative effect, in the physical exhaustion and psychological letdown of getting back to your humdrum routine (and that's before the credit card bills arrive). To achieve a love beyond words, you have to nurture *small moments* of connection day by day.

As we have explained, you can feel connected whenever you want, simply by *choosing* to feel connected. You can even do it in your head, if your partner is unavailable. You can do it when you're irritated with your partner just as easily as when you're enraptured with him or her—if you truly *want* to. And why would you want to if he's acting like a jerk or she's being a nag? Well, for one thing, he's less likely to act like a jerk if he feels connected to you, and she's less likely to nag if she knows that you care about her feelings. But the more important reason is that *you like yourself more* when you feel connected to people you love than when you don't. You like yourself more when you are nice to your partner than when you're not. You like yourself more when you are true to the most important things about you than when you are not.

One of the most destructive phrases to emerge from modern therapy and self-help books is "getting your needs met" or its variation "What about *me*?" These little words, and the self-centered attitudes they represent, have done more to promote entitlement and resentment and less to nurture love, compassion, and connection than just about anything that has passed for relationship advice. They fly in the face of a known law of human interaction: You must give what you expect to get. If you want compassion, you have to be compassionate; if you want love, you have to be loving; if you want cooperation, you have to be cooperative; if you want appreciation, you have to be appreciative day by day.

The Nightly Shame and Fear Shakeout

Here is something small but powerful that you can do *every night* to wash out the remnants of hidden shame and fear that may have accumulated during the day. It's a simple, *nightly embrace* to transform fear and shame. But it does *not* count toward your six times six hugs per day; it will likely go on for more than six seconds.

While in each other's arms, try to feel the fear under your stress, anxiety, or depression. Feel the sense of failure hiding under the tension, demands, resentment, or the doldrums of the day. Don't try to talk. Just allow the warmth of the embrace to wash out every sliver of fear and shame. Soothe

COMPASSION
CONNECTION

and be soothed. Let the embrace convince you that your connection is more important than whatever you're afraid of and whatever causes you shame.

The most profound moments between two people occur when their emotions resonate, soothing their different vulnerabilities and raising their hearts to simple enjoyment. When emotional connection goes deeper than talking, women overcome the stifling limitations of their anxieties, and men abandon destructive shame-avoiding behavior. The best protections from fear and shame are compassion, appreciation, and a sense of connection that is so deep, flexible, and resilient that it creates love beyond words.

index